Religion on Capitol Hill

Myths and Realities

Religion on Capitol Hill

Myths and Realities

□

Peter L. Benson and
Dorothy L. Williams

1817

Harper & Row, Publishers, San Francisco

Cambridge, Hagerstown, New York, Philadelphia
London, Mexico City, São Paulo, Sydney

All Bible quotations are from The New English Bible, © The Delegates of the Oxford University Press and The Syndics of the Cambridge University Press, 1961, 1970.

RELIGION ON CAPITOL HILL: *Myths and Realities.* Copyright © 1982 by Search Institute. All rights reserved. Printed in the United States of America. No part of this book may be used or reproduced in any manner whatsoever without written permission except in the case of brief quotations embodied in critical articles and reviews. For information address Harper & Row, Publishers, Inc., 10 East 53rd Street, New York, NY 10022. Published simultaneously in Canada by Fitzhenry & Whiteside, Limited, Toronto.

FIRST EDITION

Library of Congress Cataloging in Publication Data

Benson, Peter L.
RELIGION ON CAPITOL HILL.

Includes index.
1. United States. Congress—Religion. 2.United States. Congress—Voting. 3. Religion and politics—United States. I. Williams, Dorothy Lowe. II. Title
JK1140.B46 1982   328.73'073   82-47738
ISBN 0-06-060780-7

82 83 84 85 86 10 9 8 7 6 5 4 3 2 1

To Merton P. Strommen,
pioneer in research on religion,
colleague, and friend

Contents

Preface

T H I S B O O K is the latest in a procession of research projects on religion completed during Search Institute's twenty-three-year history. During that time Search Institute, an independent and non-profit research group based in Minneapolis, has had considerable experience in using the tools of the social sciences to explore the connections between people's religious beliefs and their attitudes, values, and behaviors. One of our consistent discoveries has been that religion is powerfully related to behavior. Our present discoveries echo this theme, showing that knowledge about people's religion adds importantly to an understanding of who they are and why they behave as they do.

Since writers' choice of language conveys something not only about the topic but about the writers, two language choices invite explanation. We use the word *myth* in its popular, everyday sense of "something accepted as truth without careful investigation or critical thought." We are aware of, but in this book consciously set aside, the meaning of *myth* familiar to theologians and sociologists, to whom it represents a story that expresses or explains a basic truth. We tried less ambiguous alternatives but were finally persuaded that no alternative had quite the euphony and force of *myth*.

Congressman, a word that at first seemed indispensable in writing about a study of Congress, did not accord with our preference for inclusive language. We therefore use the word *member* when referring to members of the House of Representatives and Senate, except where the reference is to someone specific who is male.

The completion of this project represents the remarkable commitment of a great many people to the idea that it is important to know more about the religious beliefs and values of members of the U.S. Congress.

First in the chronology would come the members of Search Institute's board of directors who generated, at one of their regular meetings, the audacious and exciting idea for a study of the religious beliefs held by those who make the laws of the land.

The project would have been impossible without its funders —most prominently the National Endowment for the Humanities, but also the foundations and individuals whose gifts, large and small, released matching funds so that the research could be completed and this book written. Much appreciation is extended to Lutheran Brotherhood, who sustained the project with a significant grant and whose data processing facilities were made available as part of a larger grant extended to Search Institute over a period of years.

The nine members of our advisory committee in Washington generously gave of their time and advice to the project, and commended us to a number of their colleagues in the Senate and House. That assistance was invaluable. We were also substantially aided by former congressman Burt Talcott and former Congressman (now Minnesota Governor) Albert Quie in making our requests for interview time visible and credible among many of their former colleagues.

High on the list of crucial contributions is the cooperation of the eighty members who found time to devote to the interview in spite of their already crowded schedules. We are deeply grateful for their generosity and for their willingness to let us explore with them what many of them consider very private territory.

James Dittes of Yale University and Martin Marty of the University of Chicago provided important counsel in the development of the groundwork definitions necessary to the formation of the interview. Sheridan P. McCabe of the University of Notre Dame brought considerable expertise in interviewing to his work as congressional interviewer; he also made insightful and creative contributions to the interview.

C. Gilbert Wrenn lent wisdom and counsel gleaned from his extensive writing and editing career to the formation of final drafts of several chapters. We also express our thanks to a number of other readers who gave careful attention to portions of the book dealing with matters in which they have special expertise. They are Catherine L. Albanese, Department of Religion, Wright State University; Aage Clausen, Department of Political Science, Ohio State University; Kent Eklund, political scientist and Commissioner of the Department of Energy, Planning and Development of the State of Minnesota; Erling Jorstad, Department of History, St. Olaf College; and Dennis Simon, Department of Political Science, University of Minnesota.

As is true of most Search Institute projects, this project rests on the involvement of nearly every staff member. First and foremost, of course, is the pervasive and supportive influence of the institute's president, Merton P. Strommen, who wrote the proposal, nurtured the project through the funding process, and provided important counsel on the method and scope of the research and the interpretation of the findings.

Daniel O. Aleshire carried responsibility for the project in its early months and set it on a firm conceptual foundation. Milo L. Brekke gave valuable assistance with the development of the categories of religious belief and with the development of the interview. Jan Mills served dependably and faithfully as project secretary in the early stages.

Carolyn Eklin not only served on the interview coding team but also offered incisive criticisms of several chapters. Eileen Gavin achieved the status of an honorary staff member when she devoted generous portions of her sabbatical from the College of St. Catherine to providing background literature reviews, coding interviews, offering constructive counsel, and repeatedly reviving our flagging spirits with her unfailing enthusiasm.

Phillip Wood spent many late-night and early-morning hours at the computer terminal marshaling a formidable mass of data into coherent and interpretable form. Jean Wachs typed swiftly and cheerily through the repetitive tasks of writing and rewriting, chiding and warning when our prose was cloudy, and cheering us on when the clouds lifted and meaning came clear.

We are further grateful to the Search Institute staff who erected a protective barrier between us and phone calls, routine office decisions, and committee meetings, and who took over responsibility for several major tasks that should have been ours in order to free us for the final three-month sprint toward publication.

And, finally, we appreciatively acknowledge the patience of our families, who like us better when we aren't writing books.

The information and ideas presented in this book are the result of the collaboration and support of many, to all of whom we are sincerely grateful. Such errors as appear are our own.

PETER L. BENSON
DOROTHY L. WILLIAMS

Search Institute, Minneapolis
March, 1982

1. Religion in Congress: An Issue for the 1980s

P R O B A B L Y no institution exerts a more penetrating influence on the lives of Americans, individually and corporately, than the United States Congress. In the hands of this body of 535 men and women lies the power to set laws and policies that govern daily life in America and affect the unfolding patterns of world history.

Given their enormous influence, we know surprisingly little about members of Congress as a whole. A handful of local members of Congress may be known to us, but the group fades into shadow. What are they like, these people whom we elect to govern us? What is important to them? What motivates them? How do they think about their work? How do they make their choices?

In nearly all past studies that have inquired into the identity, activity, and motivations of Congress, one area has remained almost entirely unexplored: the area of religion. Almost nothing is known about the religious beliefs and values of members. The omission is not surprising. Until about 1980 the words *religion* and *Congress* were rarely uttered in the same sentence. Except for those historians who chart the evolution of our church-state policies or those who lobby for religious organizations, almost no one associated the two words.

But that day of separation is gone. Religion and the U.S. Congress have now been publicly linked by a series of recent events. The religious stances of a number of senators and representatives have become visible to the public because of continuing controversy over two legislative issues—school prayer and abortion. New Christian Right groups like the Moral Majority have sprung vigorously into national politics, attributing virtue and tendering support to those in Congress whose voting records coincide with what the group defines as a moral position. This massive entry of religiously motivated groups into politics has raised new and profound questions about the ties between politicians' religious orientations and their political decision making.

Pope John Paul II entered the scene from a different point of view, announcing that Catholic priests ought not to seek elective office, and focusing new attention on questions about the interrelationship of sacred and secular. Two successive presidents, Carter and Reagan, have claimed the experience of being born again, giving new visibility to the national evangelical movement and raising questions about its role in government. On the world scene events like the Iranian capture of the American hostages and the ruling of Iran by a priest-led party drew new images of the mixture of political conviction and religious belief abroad in the world. The convergence of all these events of recent history has caused a surge of public interest in how religion and politics intermingle in society and particularly in government.

It was just before this surge of public concern that we embarked on a scientific journey to chronicle the religious beliefs and values held by the members of the United States Congress, and to track how they connect with the legislative decisions of Congress. This book is written to describe and discuss some of those newly identified, surprisingly strong, and broadly influential connections.

The idea for the project was conceived in 1975. The project came to life in 1978 when the National Endowment for the Humanities funded it with a major research grant.* Our original motivations were scholarly: we wanted to contribute new knowledge about the interrelationship of religion and human action as these are manifested in the U.S. Congress. We thought that scholars and professionals in the fields of religion, history, sociology, political science, education, and psychology

---

* Grant No. RO-0211-77.

would be interested in our work. We hoped also to make our discoveries intelligible and important to people in the general public who are interested in national political life, religion, or both.

The expedition turned into more of an adventure than we had bargained for. Suddenly we discovered ourselves traveling in a war zone, the area alive with crisscrossing charge and countercharge. Soberly following our scholarly instincts, we had strolled innocently onto emotion-charged turf. In the spring of 1980, at about the time the two interviewers were moving from office to office administering the congressional interview that provides the data for our research, the Moral Majority and other conservative religious groups became highly vocal and visible across the nation, and we realized how potentially explosive were the questions with which we were dealing. We began then to listen for the ways people in America perceived religion in Congress.

Six Myths about Religion in Congress

In our listening we detected six perceptions, some coming from one segment of the population and some from many quarters. We altered our plans slightly so that we could discover the accuracy of the six claims. These are the six:

1. The U.S. Congress is a hotbed of secular humanism, agnosticism, and atheism.
2. Members of Congress are less religious than the people they serve.
3. Political conservatives are more religious than political liberals.
4. Members' religious beliefs and values bear little relationship to how they vote on specific issues, except for a few select areas like abortion and school prayer.
5. Evangelical Christians in Congress are a united conservative political force.
6. Members of Congress who affirm basic Christian fundamentals adopt the politically conservative position of the New Christian Right; members who are atheists or secular humanists are politically liberal.

Our data show that all six are wrong. We will deal with each as they fit into the story of the scientific journey on which we originally set out. The story relates the experience of interviewing a representative sample of eighty senators and representatives about their deepest religious beliefs and values, what we found, and what that tells us about Congress, our nation, and ourselves.

A New View of Congress

This study presents a more stable, more human, in some ways more encouraging picture of Congress than the American public has seen before. Except for occasional magazine or television interviews with individual members, or the occasional highly publicized scandal, we have little news of Congress apart from their political stances and activities. The 535 members of Congress are too numerous for the nation to know their individual tastes, enthusiasms, and idiosyncracies as we know, for instance, the president's. Their tenure on the national scene is often too fleeting for us to acquire, over time, a sense of their temper and mood as a corporate body, as we can for the more stable membership of the Supreme Court. Visible as they seem, their identity as a group is blurred by numbers and motion, and is too ephemeral to let the average citizen develop by observation and intuition a sense of their corporate personality.

A New View of Religion

Traditionally, studies of religious beliefs have used rather global assessments. The people under investigation have been divided into those who accept the basic tenets of the Christian religion and those who do not, or into categories of Protestant, Catholic, Jewish, or into groups that differ in frequency of attendance at church or synagogue.

We approached this study believing that individuals' personal involvement with religion is more complex than that. To get at this complexity, we devised new methods for exploring religion, ones which reach deeper inside a person to discover how religion is experienced and what it means. One method was to assess the degree to which eight religious themes were present within each member's religious world-view. These eight themes are: vertical, horizontal, releasing, restricting, comforting, challenging, agentic (self-oriented), and communal. We then identified six different combinations of these themes, which we describe as religious types. The themes and types are discussed in detail in Chapter 8.

In this book we present a detailed portrait of the religious beliefs and values of members of Congress. We look for the points of commonality and the religious issues which divide. Six chapters are devoted to presenting and interpreting this portrait. The end result for the reader, we believe, will be a clearer perception of the quality and depth of the religious component in congressional life and thinking.

A New View of Religion and Voting

Religion and politics mix in the United States Congress. This fact is well known to insiders—those current or former members who have had the opportunity to observe how senators and representatives make important legislative decisions.[1] To outsiders the mix has not been visible, nor even seriously contemplated, at least until recently. Still, one wonders why political scientists who study congressional voting behavior, trying to ascertain the factors that influence voting, have not paid religious beliefs and values serious attention. At best we have an occasional study which tracks how members of different religious affiliations vote on issues like abortion.[2] But the religious-belief–voting connection is mostly unexplored territory. Few have been willing to take a hard look at it. We do not know what accounts for this inhibition. It reflects, in part, a general tendency in the social sciences to ignore religion, to pretend that it is something too ephemeral or inconsequential to consider as a force capable of shaping or informing human behavior. Merton Strommen, who reviewed all social-science doctoral dissertations completed over a twenty-five-year period, found that only 2 percent examined the role religion plays in human life.[3]

In researching this area we knew that we entered a trackless forest. Such maps as were available were based more on speculation and reflective wisdom than on sound and complete research data. We entered the forest, quite simply, in the interest of developing more distinct, accurate, and authoritative maps.

Our attempts to develop these maps led us to address four questions: Are there discernible, predictable, and systematic patterns between members' religious views and voting? How strong are the religion–voting connections? What religious beliefs and values are most closely linked to voting choices? What are the religious beliefs and values which distinguish political conservatives and liberals?

In answering these questions, we show that religious beliefs are tied in important and understandable ways to eight major legislative issues: they are strongly associated with members' stands on abortion, military expenditures, civil liberties, government spending, foreign aid, hunger relief, free enterprise, and private ownership of business and industry.

How Authentic? How Valid?

Certain legitimate questions inevitably arise about this study. Two of them are, Didn't members tell you what they wanted you to hear? and How long will this information be of use to anyone? Both questions are worth answering at the outset.

Didn't members of Congress tell you what they wanted you to hear? The hazard of eliciting the socially desirable response is a problem not new to anyone engaged in social-science research. Search Institute has a long history of developing and analyzing responses to questions administered both in written questionnaires and in oral interviews. That experience has yielded an acute awareness of the problem as well as a few methods for dealing with it.

There would certainly be considerable desire on the part of members to want to "look good," in spite of the fact that both anonymity and confidentiality were pledged. Wouldn't members, perhaps from force of habit, be inclined to maintain a "good" image for constituents, for the interviewer, or even for themselves? We purposely devised questions which would minimize this problem.

On a few questions, principally those which ask directly about the degree of the member's participation in overtly religious activities (e.g., church attendance, frequency of prayer, church leadership), what "looks good" is obvious. However, on many of the questions, it is difficult to determine quickly—or even deliberately, if one had the time—what is a socially desirable response. What is the socially desirable response to a question such as, What is the path to salvation (as the interviewee has defined *salvation*)? How should one answer these questions in order to look good: Is God changing or changeless? Does God reward and punish people for their actions? Or, If you had the power to change one thing in society, what would it be? A look through the interview questions makes it clear that social desirability could have very little influence on responses, since the questions so seldom deal with issues to which there are easily recognizable "good" responses.

The reactions of the four professionals who listened to and coded the taped interviews dealt another blow to the social-desirability hypothesis. These four—each skilled and experienced in interviewing and aware of signals that indicate when responses are genuine and when faked or distorted—overwhelmingly agreed that social desirability was not a major problem in this study.[4]

But isn't this information ephemeral? How long will it be valid? The interviews were conducted during 1980, in the latter days of the Ninety-sixth Congress. Do our conclusions hold true for the Ninety-seventh and later Congresses? First, there is only minor turnover in Congress following each national election. More than 80 percent of those who served in the Ninety-sixth Congress (1978–80) also served in the Ninety-seventh (1980–82). It is doubtful that the relatively small number of new members in each Congress alters the religious character of the whole body substantially. What might change over a long period of time is the proportion of members who fall into the six religious types. We expect that the relationship we found between religion and voting will remain fairly stable across time.

In telling the story of our journey of discovery, we have tried to include detail enough to make the work meaningful to serious students of both religion and political science, but also to explain what we found in language intelligible to the reader who has no special knowledge of either. We do not want our discoveries buried. But they will take on life only when they enter the minds and decision-making processes of people of all walks of life—those whose interest is primarily in religion, those whose interest is primarily in politics, and those who combine the two. There are increasing numbers of those who know they cannot escape the influence of both, nor the influence of forces that would now manipulate the two in order to achieve political power.

2. Interviewing Members of Congress: An Uncommon Success Story

IN ENTERING upon this study we had several things in our favor. Search Institute had over twenty years of history in national research on matters related to religious belief and values. We had staff members and consultants with both expertise in the measurement of religious belief and the conviction that, whereas most other researchers had produced rather global and relatively superficial indicators of religious behavior and belief among members of Congress, the subject could be probed in depth.

However, the greatest thing in our favor may have been a certain degree of innocence about the obstacles in the path we proposed to take. Every new turn in the road revealed yet another obstacle to be overcome.

How Does One Define *Religion*?

In setting out on a study of Religion on Capitol Hill, we found our first obstacle lurking in the first word. What is *religion*? In order to work in the area of religious belief, either we had to select one of the multitude of definitions of religion available for the choosing or we had to develop a suitable one of our own. After an extensive review of the available definitions, we were persuaded that the work we proposed demanded that we develop our own.

In 1978 three noted scholars of religion were commissioned to write position papers on the definition of religion. The scholars were James Dittes of Yale University, Martin Marty of the University of Chicago, and Jonathan Z. Smith, also of the University of Chicago. These papers provided the agenda at a symposium in which ten other scholars and professionals debated the problem of defining religion. The recommendations of the writers of the papers and the discussion at the symposium, together with the reading the staff had done, resulted in the formulation of criteria for a definition of religion and of religious belief that could serve as a foundation for the research proposed. Four major criteria were adopted for the new definition:

1. It should be elastic enough to permit inclusion of non-theistic religions (religions not predicated on the assumption that a Supreme Being exists).
2. It should be narrow enough to create a territory for itself. It should describe not only what should be *in*cluded, but also what should be *ex*cluded, as, for example, excluding questions about how human beings develop physically, or the process by which the mind learns.
3. It should minimize Western, Judeo-Christian bias. It should avoid the erroneous but all-too-easy assumption, made by American researchers and the American public alike, that adherents of Judaism and Christianity comprise the total religiously oriented population in the United States, if not among all of humanity.
4. It should avoid dealing with concepts relevant only to the institutional church. It should allow room for underground religious movements, small sects, and forms of religion that are not institutionalized.

In order to make clearer some of the issues involved in the task of definition, we can consider the three sets of terms shown in table 2-1.

Most people would agree that the terms in list *A* refer to religions. However, they all belong to a single type of religion—they are *theistic* religions, based on the assumption that there is a Supreme Being, separate from the world and separate from individual persons, a Creator of the Universe who possesses power over that universe. One of the characteristics of this kind of religious thought is that it tends to split the way one sees the

Table 2-1

A	B	C
Roman Catholicism	Pantheism	Communism
Lutheranism	Theravada Buddhism	Marxism
Mormonism	Naturalistic "religions" of Dewey, Huxley, Comte, Fromm	Science
Islam		Humanism
	Theosophy	Psychoanalytic theory

world into pairs: God/not-God, sacred/profane, spiritual/material, mind/body, good/evil. Although the adherents of the types of religion listed in *A* are recognized to be in the majority in the United States, there are many Americans who adhere to one of the kinds of religion illustrated in *B*.[1] Criterion 1 urges the development of a definition of religion that would include list *B*.

List *B* includes terms that describe what most people also agree are religions; however, these are nontheistic religions. Further, they differ from the religions listed in *A* in that they originate more in Eastern thought than in Western, and they tend toward seeking unity in all things rather than toward dividing things into pairs or diverse units. These nontheistic religions have a *monistic* concept of reality, not the dualistic concept of religions in list *A*. Monists believe that all things are really part of a single reality, but that human beings are prevented from experiencing this unity by the clutter of everyday perception and their own lack of concentration, centeredness, or simplicity. The goal of the monist is to be freed from the clutter and distraction to perceive and enter that oneness. In monistic religions primary emphasis is placed on becoming one with Religious Reality, whereas in the theistic and dualistic religions most familiar to the Western world, the emphasis is on establishing a relationship with Religious Reality—which remains something other, a being outside oneself.

List *C* contains terms which have sometimes been equated with religion, as, for instance, when people have spoken of Marxism and communism "becoming" religions, in that they seem to fill the place for some of their adherents that religion fills for others. There are people now on the national scene claiming that humanism is a religion (a claim we would dispute).

If all these lists of terms are considered "religions," the topic becomes so broad that *religion* begins to become anything a person believes, regardless of what it is. In order to adhere to criterion 2, Religion should be narrow enough to create a territory for itself, we decided that the territory covered by religion ought to include the dualistic and monistic concepts of reality illustrated in lists A and B, and exclude the kinds of ideology illustrated in list C.

Criterion 4 was adopted in recognition of the fact that some of the attempts at gauging religious belief and behavior concentrate heavily on such matters as participation or leadership in the life and structure of the institutional church. Some studies have focused on such questions as, How often do you attend worship services? Have you ever held a leadership position or taught a study group in a church?—questions that assume that religions exist only in connection with an organized group of religious people. While some questions such as these were eventually asked of members of Congress, they were not assumed to be the questions of primary importance, and, in later analysis, that assumption proved to be correct.

To meet the conditions set forth—a definition broad enough to include nontheistic religions but narrow enough to exclude such things as political ideology, and a definition not biased toward Western, Judeo-Christian, and institutional forms—the following definitions of *religion* and of *religious beliefs* were finally developed.[2]

Religion (at the individual level) is the cognitions (values, beliefs, thoughts), affect (feelings, attitudes), and behaviors involved in apprehending and responding to a reality (a supernatural being or beings, force, energy, principle, absolute consciousness) that is affirmed to exist. This reality must have the following characteristics:

1. It is a reality than which nothing greater can be conceived.
2. It is not dependent on human life for its existence.
3. It is, to some degree, beyond human voluntary control.
4. It is ultimate reality in the sense that it stands behind, sustains, controls, energizes, or holds together the diverse phenomena of the natural/physical/material world.

Religious beliefs are the truth-claims one makes in apprehending and responding to his or her concept of the Religious Reality. This includes the claims made about the nature of this reality and those made about cosmos, nature, self, people, society, and history which have been shaped by the affirmation and apprehension of this reality.

This definition was then spelled out in a system of categories of religious belief. We searched for many months to discover the various religious belief categories common to all religions— whether these be formal, institutionalized religions like Judaism; or modern religious movements like Hare Krishna; or private, personal religions that have no name. We found seven categories common to all religion forms we looked at—that is, issues that any religion would have a position on.[3] It was not until these categories were outlined that it became clear what religion-related topics should be explored with members of the U.S. Congress.

In listing the categories, the abbreviation *R* is used to refer to ultimate Religious Reality. The seven major headings of these categories convey the scope of the religious territory to be explored. The following list presents the seven major headings, together with examples of the subject matter of that category.

1. *Beliefs about the nature of Religious Reality.* What is R like? What is R's name? What kind of consciousness does R possess? What power has R? Does R respond to persons?
2. *Beliefs about Religious Reality's relationship to the world.* How is R related to the world? Is R a part of the world or separate from it? Does R participate in shaping history? Does R participate in individual human life? If R is involved in human life, how does involvement occur, and when?
3. *Beliefs about the means of apprehending Religious Reality.* How does one discover, perceive, know about R? Can individuals perceive R directly, personally? Are there special persons uniquely able to apprehend R?
4. *Beliefs about salvation and paths to salvation.* What is the highest that human beings can achieve? How does one achieve "salvation"? What is "salvation" or "the perfect state" like?
5. *Beliefs about the Last Things (eschatology).* What is believed about the final destiny of the world and of individual per-

sons? How will the end of the world come? What happens after death? What becomes of the soul? How much of a person's identity is preserved after death?

6. *Beliefs about persons and society shaped by apprehension and affirmation of Religious Reality.* How do the beliefs persons hold about R shape their understanding of human experience? Are persons truly free to make choices, or are their choices predetermined? What role does R play in individual success and failure? In personal suffering?

7. *Beliefs about values, ethical principles, and responsibilities shaped by the apprehension and affirmation of Religious Reality.* What does R expect of people? What values ought to guide human choices and action? What is good and what is evil?

With the formation of this system of categories of belief, the preliminary work was completed. Now a framework was available both for inquiring into the beliefs of adherents of nontheistic religions and for probing in depth the beliefs of the Jewish and Christian members of Congress.

It is perhaps worth noting that we found no adherents of institutionalized nontheistic religions among the members we interviewed—or none, at any rate, who were aware that elements of their religious belief were nontheistic. However, the framework is at hand should it sometime be possible to interview other populations and make comparisons with Congress.

Why Explore the Religion of Congress?

The germ of the idea for this study was enunciated in 1975, the year before the U.S. Bicentennial celebration, when the relationship of our history to our present situation was much to the fore of our national consciousness. The strong belief in God that is evident in the writings of our country's founders raised the possibility of comparing those beliefs with what present-day national leaders believe.

Although the original aim of the work was also to inquire into the beliefs of the general public in the United States, funds have not thus far been available to carry out work beyond a study of the beliefs of the senators and representatives in the U.S. Congress.

Why are the beliefs of Congress of particular interest? Because these few people—535 of them, a mere handful out of the millions of U.S. citizens—have been elected by the rest of the citizenry to run the affairs of state, they take on several characteristics that make them important as subjects of a study.

To begin with, they have power. The decisions made by this handful of people affect the lives of the rest of us daily, perhaps hourly. They make decisions that set the social and economic conditions under which we live and work. They decide how much of the money we earn must be paid as taxes to the federal government; they decide how our national resources are to be used. They regulate our relations with the rest of the world—whether we feed certain groups of people, and whether we make war with certain others. They influence the global atmosphere toward harmony and disharmony. They influence the prices we receive or pay for goods. They decide which of our rights shall be protected by law and under what conditions we shall be deprived of those rights. This relatively small group makes decisions that shape national life more intimately and directly than any other group of comparable size we can name. The more we know about them the better.

Members of Congress are also visible. Unless we are in the presence of an accomplished storyteller, information about people we don't know rarely interests us or sticks in memory. We have no frame to hang the information on. But tell us something about someone we have heard of—a television personality, a sports star—and we are all ears; we have a frame to fit it into. That is true of members of Congress. We know something about them. We hear, or half-hear, their names in newscasts; we read their names. Now and then, when they have taken a stand on an issue that matters to us particularly, we may even have written or spoken to them. It is easier to capture our interest with news about them because they are visible.

Further, in a way that the dramatic actor or sports star cannot be, members of Congress are symbolic of the American public. They are ourselves writ large. For reasons that are not always entirely clear, they are like us. When one or another of the candidates strikes a sympathetic chord in us, we elect that one to run a portion of our lives for us.

And yet, with all their visibility and power, they are also invisible. There is a great void of knowledge about the members of Congress. There are two major categories of things the public hears about members. One category includes their action on political issues. The other category involves individual stories about individual lives—sometimes human and heart-warming stories, but more often vignettes that have an eye-to-the-keyhole flavor, gossip and scandal splashed across the newssheets that tell us little about who the members of Congress truly are.

Group information about Congress on any nonpolitical subject is very hard to come by. Members simply do not voluntarily gather together for group portraits of any sort. Except on political business, members are almost inaccessible. In our background work for this research, we were unable to find a single study that explored with a random sample of Congress any issue that was not political in nature.

Designing the Interview

Once the definition of religion was formulated and the categories that fleshed it out were complete, the next step was to design the interview with which we would approach the unapproachable, inaccessible Congress in the hope of collecting information.

A well-constructed interview does not feel to the interviewee like an interview at all, but like a pleasant and absorbing conversation. However, behind the seemingly artless flow of questions in a carefully designed interview considerable art is concealed.

The hallmarks of a good set of research or measurement questions are *completeness, economy,* and *attractiveness.* The areas to be explored must first be chosen. Then questions must be framed, tried out, and sharpened so that information from all the desired areas is elicited (completeness), so that one does not collect an abundance of interesting but extraneous matter (economy), and so that the questions hold the interest and good will of the interviewee (attractiveness).

Four guidelines shaped the subject matter of the congressional interview. To begin with, it seemed desirable to ask questions covering all seven of the categories of belief. In this way we could develop a broad and complete portrait of what we defined religious belief to be. A second decision was to use multiple measures, sets of several questions all related to the same issue whose answers would give more solidly dependable information than answers to single questions could be expected to do. A third decision was to include some questions about membership in church or synagogue, frequency of attendance at worship, leadership roles in religious institutions, and certain religious practices or experiences, such as engaging in personal prayer or feeling that one is in the presence of God. These were included to serve as a link with information available from public polls and with other research that has focused principally on religious practices. And fourth, a decision was made to ask a number of *open-ended* questions, that is, questions for which a list of possible answers was not given, so as to make it more difficult for members to choose answers which put them in a good light rather than revealing their true sentiments.

How Does One Capture a Congressional Interview?

Early in the project a ten-member advisory committee, composed of members of both the Senate and the House, met to hear the outline of what was proposed and to offer counsel. As the committee spoke about the pressures of life in the Congress, the advice amounted to a litany of the obstacles we faced, and it went something like this.

First, the committee said, we like what you propose to do. It has not, to our knowledge, been done before, and we anticipate that good will come of it if you succeed. However:

1. Because of the extreme demand on the time of members, many have a standing rule that they will see only constituents.

2. Because this is an election year (1980), many members travel to their home districts every weekend; this further increases the pressures of time and further decreases your chances of securing interviews.

3. Most members have a standing policy against granting interviews, either oral or written. The number of requests members receive for interviews (from dissertation writers, political science students, high-school civics students, and the press)

ranges between 350 and 2,000 a year. The no-interview policy is an obvious necessity.

4. Religion is considered by many in Congress, as among the American public, to be a very personal topic, and some may refuse to cooperate on those grounds, even if other difficulties can be surmounted.

5. Members of Congress are accustomed to being informed and articulate on almost any topic. If they fear sounding less than articulate about religious subjects, they are likely to refuse.

6. Be wary of questions that will allow the person responding to choose a socially desirable response. Members of Congress do not customarily get where they are by indiscrimately saying what they think; most are adept at tailoring their conversation to suit the interests and hopes of whatever audience is before them.

In spite of these warnings of considerable difficulty ahead, we held to our original intention to work with a random sample of Congress. Work done with convenience samples—those who volunteer, or who most willingly cooperate in a survey or participate in an interview—is not highly regarded among serious researchers. Random samples are. If we were to make discoveries, we intended that they be taken seriously, and be representative of the entire 535-member Congress.

We determined that a random sample of Congress should include individuals who accurately represented the makeup of the Ninety-sixth Congress, then in session, in these categories: Republican/Democrat, region of the country, and religious affiliation as recorded in the 1980 edition of *The Almanac of American Politics*. We drew our random sample from the pool of 535 names (100 senators; 435 representatives), choosing 112 names (or about 1 of every 5), and using a special technique which ensured that the random sample satisfactorily represented those categories.4

Then the real work began—the arduous, tedious task of contacting and persuading the 112 members to consent to an interview. The caution voiced by the advisory committee began to loom large. The difficulty in gaining cooperation made us appreciate why so few social scientists pursue interview studies in

Congress. Nonetheless, we persisted, inventing new "persuasion techniques" in mid-stream. To capture the essence of our strategy, we list below some of the things we did to overcome what seemed to be insurmountable obstacles.

1. Made several visits to each member of the project advisory committee for help in designing the solicitation strategy, determining the length and style of the interview, and shaping the content of a project brochure, and to enlist the committee's cooperation in writing endorsement letters to each of the 112 members in the sample.
2. Tested an early version of the interview with some members of the project advisory committee. Reshaped and redirected questions where necessary.
3. Briefed all members of the advisory committee on the final version of the interview.
4. In March, 1980, sent the project brochure and an invitation to be interviewed to all members in the sample.
5. Saw that Dear Colleague endorsement letters from five members arrived shortly thereafter. Mailing dates of the letters were staggered so that one was received on each of several different days.
6. Engaged a former member of the House (1964–78), known and highly respected among members in both the House and the Senate, to send an endorsement letter to each of the 112, and to begin the arduous task of setting interview appointments. He worked nearly full-time during March–May, 1980, to contact each of the 112. These contacts included phone calls (often as many as ten or twelve per office), letters, and face-to-face visits.
7. Arranged for another former member of Congress to write to twenty members, each a good friend and colleague during his twenty years in the House.
8. Enlisted seven members who had completed the interview to encourage others to participate.
9. Visited the offices of forty members who had declined the first request for an interview, attempting to persuade the appointment secretary and/or other staff member to make a personal appeal for cooperation.

10. Mailed a second round of invitation letters in July, 1980, to a group that had declined the original interview.

The project brochure, sent to each member chosen in the random sample, contained information about the purposes and benefits of the study. Included were a list of safeguards, intended to minimize apprehension and to assure members that their anonymity would be preserved. We guaranteed confidentiality, promising no release of individual interview information. We promised that no data would be made available until after the 1980 elections. We guaranteed that the names of persons on the advisory committee and of those interviewed would not be released. We said that the information collected would be presented in the form of summary scores or, in the case of individuals' actual words, presented without attribution. At the time of each interview the member was asked whether he wished the tape returned or destroyed, when the analysis was complete. (Those wishes have now been carried out.)

How Successful Were We?

We were able to interview 72 percent of them, or 80 of the 112-member sample. That, in social-science research, is a respectable cooperation rate. However, since we wanted our interviews to represent the entire Congress, we checked to see how well the 80 interviewed members compared with the entire body of 535. Table 2-2 compares the characteristics of the interviewed sample with the 535. Overall, it appears that the 80 interviewed members are quite representative of the 535, at least on things we can measure.[5] Members from eastern states are slightly underrepresented in the sample, and members from the South and West are slightly overrepresented. The sample also slightly overrepresents affiliation with mainline Protestant traditions.

We also compared the eighty we interviewed to the full group of 535 on a wide range of political issues. On voting measures of political liberalism, political conservatism, support for labor, support for farmers, support for business, and support for military expenditures, the two groups were not significantly different.

Table 2-2

Characteristics	Percentage of Ninety-Sixth Congress with This Characteristic (N = 534)	Percentage of Sample with This Characteristic (N = 80)
	(Numbers Rounded to Nearest Whole Number)	
Party		
Republican	37	39
Democrat	63	61
Senate or House		
Senate	18	16
House	81	84
Region		
East	22	15
Midwest	27	26
South	30	35
West	18	24
Religious Affiliation*		
Liberal Protestant	19	15
Mainline Protestant	33	39
Conservative Protestant	13	15
Roman Catholic	24	20
Jewish	6	6
Unlisted	5	5
Sex		
Male	97	94
Female	3	6
	Average	*Average*
Age	52	51
Education (on a Five-Point Scale)	3	3
Years in Congress	10	11

*Examples of religious traditions classified as liberal, mainline, or conservative are as follows:

Liberal	Mainline	Conservative
Unitarian	Lutheran (LCA, ALC)	Lutheran Church—
Episcopal	Presbyterian	Missouri Synod
United Church	United Methodist	Southern Baptist
of Christ	African Methodist	Evangelical Free
	Episcopal	Seventh-day Adventist
	Reformed Church	Church of the Nazarene
	in America	

There is a slight possibility that the eighty who agreed to be interviewed differed systematically on some religious perspectives from the thirty-two who declined the interview. To explore this possibility we asked four longtime observers of religion on Capitol Hill to look at the names of members in the two lists. None of the four was able to detect any important differences between the two groups. Nevertheless, there is a possibility that any member who harbored strong antireligious sentiments (without having revealed these attitudes to anyone, including our four observers) would refuse to be interviewed. To be antireligious might be seen as a political liability, possibly even as anti-American. If such "closet" antireligious members exist, we would expect their number to be very small. Nonetheless, it would mean that we paint a slightly more religious picture of Congress than in truth exists. We do not believe that our portrait is faulty for this reason, but we acknowledge that the possibility exists.

Coding the Congressional Interviews

The interviews averaged thirty-five minutes in length and were tape-recorded. Most were conducted in members' offices. It is probably testimony to the interests of the interviewed members that many a member who had promised no more than fifteen minutes ignored ringing telephones and insistent aides to prolong the conversation to forty or fifty minutes.[6]

Some commented, on completion of the interview, that Congressional life does not often offer occasion to discuss religious beliefs and experiences in the depth at which the interview had probed them, and that it felt good to be invited to "talk religion" in this way.

In May of 1981 a team of four coded the interviews. Coders used both the taped recording of the interview and a typewritten transcript of the recording in making their judgments. Neither tape nor typed transcript bore the interviewee's name, party affiliation, or political orientation. The only identification evident to coders was sex and sometimes region, where it came clear in speech patterns characteristic of a particular part of the country.

A relatively complex system of coding enabled the coders to

derive approximately 124 pieces of information from the fifty interview questions (which are listed in appendix A). The coding forms for the interview ran to thirty pages, asking for judgments not only as to the content of response, but, where appropriate, as to the degree of salience, importance, or emphasis given to each answer.[7]

How the Book Is Organized

We call the 124 things on which each member is given a score *units of information*—all related to specific beliefs, values, and behaviors of each member. Chapters 3 through 7 are based on these units of information, as we develop a descriptive portrait of the kinds and varieties of religious positions that exist in Congress and how these compare with those of the public and the nation's founders.

We also wanted to know how the units of information combine into religious themes or emphases that run through a member's religious view. For example, how comforting, or challenging, or restricting is the religion? We refer to these combinations as *scales,* and developed thirteen of them. As one last step we grouped members into six different *types* of religion. The scales and types, developed through rigorous scientific methods, are described in chapter 8.

Chapters 9 and 10 discuss how each of these ways of describing religion—*units of information, scales,* and *types*—are linked to members' voting decisions.

A good deal of the charm of a task, for those involved in doing it, is to know its difficulties and to know those difficulties overcome. This was a difficult piece of research to complete. But the difficulty of a task does not necessarily determine its value. The value of the research is in handing on what was discovered, and in the effect that those handed-on discoveries have on how persons then think and act.

3. What Does Congress Believe?

> *Myth Number One:* The U.S. Congress is a hotbed of secular humanism, agnosticism, and atheism.

I N T H I S chapter we begin a portrait of the religious beliefs held by members of the U.S. Congress. Our discoveries about these beliefs cast grave doubt on the oft-voiced allegation today that Congress is overrun with secular humanists, agnostics, and atheists. There appear, on the contrary, to be a good many in Congress who are committed believers, who have thought deeply about their religious beliefs, and who can articulate those beliefs, some speaking with the comfortable ease of long familiarity with religious thought.

The portrait of beliefs held by members of Congress is presented in seven sections related to the seven categories of religious belief mentioned in chapter 2 and listed below.

1. Beliefs about the Nature of Religious Reality
2. Beliefs about Religious Reality's Relationship to the World
3. Beliefs about the Means of Apprehending Religious Reality
4. Beliefs about Salvation and Paths to Salvation
5. Beliefs about the Last Things (Eschatology)
6. Beliefs about People and Society
7. Beliefs about Values and Ethical Principles

Beliefs about the Nature of Religious Reality

An overwhelming percentage of members affirm the existence of God. At the start of the interview each member was handed a page with five statements on it. Each was asked to choose the statement that best described his or her belief. Table 3-1 lists the five statements and the percentage of members choosing each statement.

Table 3-1

Statement	Percentage Who Chose This Response
A. I don't believe in God or an ultimate Religious Reality (some power, being, force, or energy that holds things together and influences the world's destiny).	0
B. I don't think it is possible for me to know whether God or an ultimate Religious Reality exists.	1
C. I am uncertain but lean toward not believing in an ultimate Religious Reality.	4
D. I am uncertain but lean toward believing.	9
E. I definitely believe that God or some ultimate Religious Reality exists.	86

When we combine the responses to statements *D* and *E*, the percentage of our sample who at least lean toward affirming God's existence is 95 percent. Not a single person in our sample admitted to an atheistic position, though several leaned toward disbelief. One member chose *B*, the agnostic position.

The question about certainty was carefully worded to permit the affirmation of Religious Realities other than God. In Western culture the vast majority of persons use the word *God* to designate Religious Reality. Other names are possible, of course. *Brahma* and *Allah* are names used in other cultures, and among some Americans who have adopted other than a Judeo-Christian religious perspective. After hearing responses to this first question, we knew that all members in our sample referred to Religious Reality as *God*. Accordingly, we used this term throughout the rest of the interview.

We asked several questions about the attributes of God. Why several? There are two reasons. First, Religious Reality is the central figure in most, if not all, religions. Much of a person's religious belief system emanates from how one sees and experiences this central phenomenon. These perceptions color one's views of people, society, values, and moral responsibilities. Second, we know that people differ considerably in how they view God.[1] Some see God as a warm and loving companion while others see God as a remote and impersonal entity. For a minority God is stern and strict, not unlike the stereotype of the authoritarian father of Victorian England: distant, aloof, and a little disdainful. For others, God presents a gentler image, giving human beings permission to engage life as fully and completely as possible.

The fourth question of the interview was, When you think of God, what three or four qualities come to mind? Most members had little trouble coming up with several God-images. Some focused on God's power and might. Some described God's way of relating to people, mentioning such attributes as "forgiving," "loving," and "caring." And some focused on God as standard-setter or judge.

Table 3-2 lists the attributes that members mentioned. Their choices clearly reflect the fact that all members in our sample have their roots in the Judeo-Christian understanding of God. Our sample emphasized both the transcendent (distant, "out there") characteristics and the immanent (close by, present and involved) characteristics of God. These two are the standard God-images of most American religious traditions. More than 80 percent of the sample gave a mixture of transcendent and immanent images. The images associated with Eastern religions or some of the newer religious movements were absent from the members' concepts of God. Sterner images, such as "vindictive," "wrathful," and "jealous," associated with Old Testament writings, were also rarely chosen by members.

A second method we used to get at how members perceive and experience God was to present a series of twenty-one statements about God and ask how true each image or adjective was.

The twenty-one prepared statements about God offered to members are shown in table 3-3. They are listed in order from those that members declared most true to those rated least true. In this second list we see evidence of belief in a benevolent and

Table 3-2

Attribute	Number of Members (out of Eighty) Who Mentioned This Attribute*
God is transcendent	
Omnipotent, powerful	31
Omniscient (all-knowing)	22
Ruler of the universe	16
Creator	13
Not fully knowable, vast	11
Ultimate goodness	7
Omnipresent	5
Wisdom, vision	4
Holy, awesome	1
Other qualities	5
Total Transcendent	115
God is loving, benevolent	
Loving	36
Forgiving, merciful	20
Gives guidance, direction	12
Comforter, gives hope	11
Understanding	9
Helpmate, companion, friend	4
Dependable	1
Other qualities	3
Total Loving	96
God sets expectations, standards	
Just, expects justice	16
Judging	8
Has high standards	6
Demanding, stern	4
Total Expectations	34

*Total sums to more than eighty because some Members gave more than one response.

personal God. Only a minority view God in impersonal terms, such as "distant," "in my life more as a symbol than as a real presence I can feel," and "unapproachable."

For the majority of members God is real, a personally felt presence. For some the relationship is a part of everyday life. More than half affirm that "God is my constant companion,"

Table 3-3

Statement	Percentage Who Said Statement Is True
God is faithful and dependable	87
God is all-powerful	87
God is both awesome and fascinating	84
God is aware of everything I think and do	75
God is close	74
God is a being who has a will, consciousness, and feelings	72
God is always just and fair	70
God is forgiving	69
God accepts me as I am	67
God is mysterious	66
God liberates me, sets me free	62
God is my constant companion	53
God is clearly knowable	52
God has a plan for my life	48
God is strict	47
God is permissive	28
God is best understood as a spirit, force, or process	24
God is in my life more as a symbol than as a real presence I can feel	23
God, like people, is constantly evolving and changing	20
God is distant	12
God is unapproachable	6
God is more present in community and relationships than in individual lives	5
God is vindictive	0

and three-fourths say that "God is aware of everything I think and do."

To this point we have been discussing how the eighty-member sample responded to each of many images of God, taken one at a time. What are the combinations of beliefs about God held by members? To look at this question we used a sophisticated analytical technique called cluster analysis to help us discern how beliefs about God are packaged. We used information from the twenty-one how-true-about-God statements and the open-ended question about God described earlier.

We discovered three general concepts or images of God in the minds of the U.S. legislators. About 95 percent of our sample described God in terms that fall into one of the three image categories described below. The three images share a common core: members believe that God has a loving, caring, and protective attitude toward the world. Beyond this, however, the images diverge.

Attentive-Parent God

The largest proportion of members (about 40 percent) believe in a God who is like the attentive parent of an almost grown child. The parent is aware of the child, is deeply interested in the child's welfare, but stands somewhat removed, encouraging the development of freedom and independence. In this kind of relationship the parent may choose to intervene only in certain special circumstances of particular need or to challenge the child to take some new direction. A large number of members of Congress describe God as being somewhat like that, an attentive parent: aware, caring, perhaps intervening sporadically, but not directly involved in the guidance of every moment, every decision.

Companion God

A second God-image brings God more constantly inside one's life. God is more than accessible; God is always there, working as a partner. As one hears the relationship described, God and individual do not seem coequals in the companionship. God is out front, pulling the believer along, running interference, steering the believer in desirable directions. One gives over one's life to this protecting companion, trusting that God knows what is best. Most members in this type assert that they gain a sense of freedom and liberation by surrendering their lives to God. Through the act of surrender comes an assurance that one is cared for and a confidence that all perils will be overcome. Approximately 25 percent of our sample espouses this kind of individual God-image.

Abstract God

Members who hold the third God-image minimize the degree to which God relates to individual persons. God's presence and activity is less evident to this group, less immediately experienced. This Abstract God image is a mostly intellectual concept: contact with God is more an exercise of the mind than of the heart. Most members in this group view God as mysterious and too vast, too complex to be fully grasped by finite minds.

There are two different forms of the Abstract God concept. One group sees God as abstract and absent, both from the member's personal life and from any of life that the member can perceive. The other sees God as abstract and involved. Members who describe this image do not push God to the outer edges of life. They see God as active, but not as constantly or closely present in the personal lives of individuals as for those who describe the Companion God and Attentive-Parent God images. Approximately 30 percent of the sample falls into the Abstract God category, with about 15 percent falling into each of the two subgroups.

Beliefs about Religious Reality's Relationship to the World

We have seen that God, for most members, is immanent—God is in the world, active in its affairs. In this section we will attempt to define the way legislators understand this activity.

The question of God's activity in the world raises an important philosophical issue about the nature of reality. To say that God is active implies that there are two different realities—the sphere of natural reality (people, other forms of life, the physical universe) and Religious Reality (or God). To say that God is active in the lives of people or in physical events implies that God enters the natural sphere but is at the same time separate from or independent of this natural order. Another is the monistic position, described in chapter 2, that there is only one reality. The natural world is not separate from God but is part of God. God, then, *is* the world or, alternatively, the world is God. If one holds this belief, the question of God's activity in the world is nonsense, for, by implication, the activity of people and the physical world is God's activity. This kind of thinking seems absurd to some people, but it is well entrenched in both historical and contemporary Eastern cultures, most notably in countries with Hindu or Buddhist traditions. Even in this country the premise that God and the world are one has significant support.[2]

Beliefs about God's relationship to the world have six different variants. Immediately following our question about the existence of God, we handed the interviewee a sheet giving a brief definition of each of the six variants and an illustrative diagram, asking that the member choose the picture that symbolized God's relationship to the world. The definitions and diagrams are given in table 3-4. Positions *A* and *B* represent the one-reality view. Positions *D, E,* and *F* represent the two-realities view. Position *C* is a hybrid of these two, which holds that people are part of God but that other aspects of the natural sphere are not.

Position *A*, God and the world are one, is often called *pantheism*.[3] In this system there is only one reality. The universe is God, and God is the universe. The following definition nicely captures the essence of pantheism:

Pantheism is the theory which regards all finite things as merely aspects, modifications, or parts of one eternal and self-existent being; which views all material objects and all particular minds as necessarily derived from a single infinite substance. The one absolute substance— the one all-comprehending being—it calls God. Thus God, according to it, is all that is; and nothing is which is not essentially included in, or which has not been necessarily evolved out of God.[4]

Pantheism has considerable psychological appeal, for it follows that if God is good, then people and the world, being part of God, are also good.

Position *B*, The world is part of God, but God is greater and larger than the world, shares with pantheism the notion that there is only one reality. However, God is not identical to the universe, as in pantheism, but at the same time both includes the world and is transcendent to it. This position is called *panentheism*.[5]

Positions *D, E,* and *F* all assume that there are two realities— God and the natural world. These three differ in the degree to which God becomes involved in the natural world. Position *D*, God set the world in motion but does not play an active role in the world, is called *deism*. This point of view had its major roots

Table 3-4

Statement	Percentage Who Chose This Response
A. God and the world are one.	4

B. The world is part of God, but God is greater and larger than the world.	26

C. Human beings are part of God.	5

D. God sets the world in motion but does not play an active role in the world.	3

E. God transcends the world, entering the world infrequently.	5

Table 3-4 *(cont.)*

Statement	Percentage Who Chose This Response
F. God transcends the world but is actively involved in the world.	37
G. Combinations and other responses.	21

in the seventeenth and eighteenth centuries, a period of time often referred to as the Age of Reason or the Enlightenment.

Position *F* is called *theism.* God transcends the world but is also actively involved in it. God acts upon it, intervenes, makes things happen. There are many views of the arenas in which God acts. Possibilities include history, physical nature—as in the case of some miracles—society, and individual lives. Theism is the cornerstone of all major Judeo-Christian religious traditions. If there is anything in common in the official theologies of Jewish, Catholic, and Protestant thought, it is that God simultaneously stands above the universe and acts in and through it. Position *E* is a reduced form of theism, differing from *F* only in the perception of how often, or to what degree, God is involved with the world.

Position *C,* Human beings are a part of God, is an interesting mixture of the one-reality (*A* and *B*) and two-reality (*D, E,* and *F*) views. Only that part of the world composed of people is considered part of God. Presumably, God stands outside the rest of creation and has the ability to act on it—a position not unlike what theists affirm.

How do the members of Congress divide among these six different views? Over a third chose the theism option. This figure is somewhat surprising, given that theism is so often assumed to be the overwhelmingly dominant orientation in the

Western world. Only two members chose deism. The rationale given for this choice is particularly interesting. Both members reported that they were theists until something tragic happened in their lives. Not being able to reconcile an immanent and benevolent God with the occurrence of capricious misfortune, they took God out of the world as a way of resolving the inconsistency. One of these "deists" said, "I used to have a firmer belief in God. But a couple of years ago someone I cared about very much was killed in a car crash. That really shook me. If God really loves us, why would he let that happen? I just don't understand. I try, but I just can't figure it out."

The second largest group of members (26 percent) chose what we identified as the *panentheistic* view. Did the members who chose this response know what they were doing? This is not a position espoused by most religious traditions. Perhaps the selection simply reflected a lack of clarity in or commitment to one's beliefs. If one really meant something by this choice, we would expect other beliefs, theologically consistent with panentheism, also to be affirmed. For example, a person who interprets the world as actually being part of God ought to have a particularly high estimate of human nature and a more generous conception of the possibility of salvation. It seems inconsistent to say that some of God's children, being part of his/her actual being, will perish after death. Indeed, when we compare the panentheists in our sample with the theists, we find that the former do have a more benevolent view of human nature and a more generous estimate of the percentage of people who will "be saved." Apparently the panentheistic view is a meaningful choice for some members.

We have established that, for most members, God's presence in the world is a given. For some the world is part of God, and for others God is a being separate from the world who chooses to get involved. Where do members find God's involvement most visible? Is it in history? In society? In individual lives? Table 3-5 summarizes members' responses.

Nearly all the interviewees affirmed that God is a creative force in history, though we are not sure that people would find it easy to explain exactly what this means. The second state-

Table 3-5

Statement	Percentage Who Gave This Response
God is a creative force in history.	
True	88
Not sure	8
False	4
God works to protect and preserve our social institutions and structures.	
True	34
Not sure	8
False	58

ment, God works to protect and preserve our social institutions and structures, provoked a wider range of responses. About one-third saw this as at least somewhat true, while nearly all others saw it as false. The editorial comments that members offered on the question about social institutions yielded some further information. Only 22 percent actually conceived of God as directly supporting the American social system. A larger percentage (32 percent) saw God as having social expectations, but working through individuals to accomplish these purposes. A small number (6 percent) appeared to have caught the conservative implication of the question and offered the alternative view that God is about the business of transforming, not preserving, the social system. This 6 percent might have been considerably higher had the interviewers more actively probed members' reasons for disagreeing with the question as it was stated.

An equally varied set of perspectives was elicited by this statement: In their lifetime God sometimes punishes those who are evil and rewards those who are good. The vote was split: approximately 40 percent agreed, and 40 percent disagreed. We are not sure what form members think these rewards and punishments take. Apparently wealth is not considered one of the possible rewards. Only 3 percent of our sample found any truth in the statement that wealth is a sign of God's favor.

There is historical significance to this finding. Max Weber, the noted sociologist, thought that capitalism flourished in

America partly because of Calvinist religious ideas particularly prominent in early American history.[6] His reasoning goes like this. Many early Americans adopted the view that God predestined some to eternal life and some to eternal damnation. People were highly motivated to figure out whether or not they were one of God's chosen few. What evidence could they use? Presumably, those who were blessed with wealth or position could take this as a sign of having been chosen. Accordingly, Weber said, people would strive for wealth and, once attaining it, perceive it as a "sign of God's favor." The accuracy of this hypothesis is still being debated.[7] If Weber is right about this early American reasoning, then we can presume that agreement with the interview's statement about wealth might have been more strongly affirmed at an earlier point in our history.

The beliefs we have been considering thus far represent somewhat simplistic notions of causation and are about people in general. The beliefs people hold about God's role in their own lives are more complex, often involving some kind of interaction between God and the self. To get a picture of God "in my life," we combed each interview for relevant statements and then placed each member in one of eight different categories of how God operates "in my life." (See table 3-6.)

Only one member holds the position that God is in charge of absolutely everything that happens. At the other extreme we find that 11 percent of members believe God is not involved in the conduct of one's life. Between these extremes we have a range of statements about how God and persons interact. The major difference is between those who listen for God's plan and attempt to act according to that plan and those who are on their own in life but aware of God's expectations. This difference is reminiscent of our earlier discussion of types of God-concepts (Companion, Attentive-Parent, Abstract). Indeed, the members who hold a Companion God concept tend to be at the upper end (responses 1, 2, and 3) of the categories, attributing to God a strong and active role in their personal lives. The Attentive-Parent God members are located in two different places. Forty-five percent are in the God-has-put-us-in-charge-of-our-lives

Table 3-6

Statement	Percentage Who Gave This Response
1. God is in charge of everything that happens in my life.	1
2. God has a plan for my life. If I listen to God, the plan will become known to me, and then I can act on it.	29
3. God is not automatically in charge of persons' lives. But if I ask God for help and direction, he will enter my life and help direct me. (Constant.)	9
4. I am in charge of my own life, but God will give me help if I ask him. (Sporadic.)	9
5. God may have a plan for my life, or may be in my life, but I'm not sure.	6
6. God has put us in charge of our own lives. We are able to make our own mistakes. I am on my own, but I am aware of what God hopes we will be and what he expects from us.	28
7. God has put us in charge of our own lives. Because he loved me, I am in the world with a certain attitude.	6
8. I am in charge of my life. God is not involved directly or indirectly.	11

category, while 39 percent share the Companion God perception that God and persons are partners in pursuing God's grand design.

Beliefs about the Means of Apprehending Religious Reality

Where does one look for God? God is not as directly accessible to the senses as, say, the neighbor next door or the lamppost on the corner. This has been a lively theological question for centuries. In fact, history has sometimes turned on this issue. Some claim that the Reformation in Europe in Martin Luther's time had much to do with Luther's contention that the common man and woman did not need professional clergy to bring them and God together.

Some of the open-ended questions in the interview were particularly difficult for members to handle. One learns much from this kind of question, for it provides not only information about the actual verbal response, but also information about the ease with which it is answered—immediate response, or silence, shifting in the chair, a sigh. One of these difficult questions was, If you wanted to help someone who did not believe in God to find God, where would you tell him or her to look? Inside oneself? In Scripture? In nature? Or where? How do we know this question was difficult to answer? In the first place, more than half of the members gave only one response—and it was usually one of the three examples we gave (nature, Scripture, and self). The response usually came with no embellishment and no editorial comment, though we purposely gave adequate time for additional responses and/or explanations. A minority of members gave multiple, confident, certain responses—evidence that the issue of apprehending God was something they had thought about. (See table 3-7.)

Differing ideas about how Scripture is to be viewed have divided people for centuries. Is the Bible truly God's revealed word, or is it merely humankind's best attempt at intuiting Religious Reality? Further, if it is truly God's revealed word, is it inerrant, without error of any kind? And does *inerrant* mean that all its facts are true as stated, or only that general principles and truths are conveyed and that not all of the specific facts are to be taken as literal truth? The frequent national debate about whether the world was created or evolved bears testimony to the fact that issues related to the literal and figurative interpretation of Scripture are still alive.

Table 3-7

Statement	Percentage Who Gave This Response*
If you wanted to help someone who did not believe in God to find God, where would you tell him or her to look? In Scripture? In nature? Inside oneself? Or where?	
In nature, in creation	41
In Scripture	32
Inside oneself	29
Consult clergy or religious counselor	12
In observing other people's lives	13
In history	4
Through the church	4
Through prayer, meditation	4
Other	4
	143

*Percentages sum to more than 100 percent because some members gave more than one response.

Table 3-8 lists three units of information derived from the interview which bear on this question.

Four-fifths of members believe that Scripture is divinely revealed truth; they reject the suggestion that God was uninvolved in the writing of Scripture. God played a role in the design of Scripture, and the words therein reveal God's nature, purpose, and activity.

There is disagreement, as there would probably be with any group of people, over how far to press these claims. The first three categories of explanation as to God's role (which also sum to 80 percent) show how legislators divide. Almost all of them take the less strict view that God inspired writers or communicated the basic concepts, and that there is a human as well as a divine element in what we read in the Scriptures.

One Congressman reviewed a recent conversation with his wife, who had raised an apparent inconsistency in the story of Cain and Abel.

And I said, "Honey, you've got to remember that these are parables . . . that grew up and became frozen into the folklore. . . ." There was a

Table 3-8

Statement	Percentage Who Gave This Response
God did not play a role in the writing of Scripture.	
True	7
Not sure	13
False	80
Explanation of the role God played in writing Scripture (comments following the preceding question).	
God dictated Scripture	4
God inspired writers	51
God communicated the basic concepts and ideas, and people took it from there	25
God played no role	7
Other	13
Everything in Scripture is absolutely true and factual.	
True	23
Not sure	6
False	71

great flood once. Now, whether or not the animals walked two by two and climbed on board and were saved and a new world started, . . . a person can believe that if he wants to. But we've had ice ages and there isn't one mentioned in the Bible; isn't that strange?

This Congressman, at the same time that he cast doubt on the literal truth of Scripture, affirmed the truth of the basic concepts conveyed in Scripture. He expressed the same general attitude of another who said that though he believed that God communicated the Ten Commandments to Moses, it didn't matter to him whether they were inscribed on stone, printed on Xerox paper, or whispered in Moses' ear—he still regarded the Ten Commandments as part of God's will.

Comparison of the beliefs of Congress on this question with the beliefs of the American public will be made in chapter 5, and further comment made on the issue of inerrancy.

Institutional religion usually plays to mixed reviews. There has always been a segment of the population who stayed away from the church, seeing in it more hindrance than help. The members of Congress, by and large, have moderately favorable views toward the church. Asked whether they "come to know

God better through the church," three-quarters answered affirmatively. On the other hand, nearly one-half also saw at least some truth in the statement, The church often inhibits the development of mature religious faith. Why the discrepancy? There are at least two possibilities. First, perhaps the know-God-better question was interpreted as being about the interviewee, specifically, while the inhibits-development question was interpreted as being about people in general. Equally plausible is this: God and faith are not the same thing. The church can help one find God, but when a church adds in all the other trappings—the rituals, the money, the potluck dinners—the faith, in its general sense, gets watered down. (In chapter 4 we will see to what extent members actually get involved in church life.)

Jesus is, of course, the cornerstone of Christianity, the personage some consider to be God's most perfect revelation, providing the best window through which to apprehend God. Do members of Congress believe that Jesus is divine, or human, or both? And what personal meaning does Jesus have for them? We asked each member, "Who was Jesus?" We probed until we were able to establish the member's beliefs about Jesus' divinity and humanity. The results are shown in table 3-9.

Table 3-9

Statement	Percentage Who Gave This Response
Jesus was both divine and human	68
Jesus was divine but not human	3
Jesus was human, not sure about divinity	16
Jesus was human but not divine	13

Overall, 71 percent affirmed the divinity of Jesus. This is about the same percentage that Stark and Glock found in their national study of the beliefs of Protestants and Catholics.[8] We also asked, "What does Jesus mean to you?" The following four quotes, each from different members, capture the range of replies:

Well, I think that Jesus is a role model for us. I think that his life, if emulated, can be very worthwhile.

Jesus was the mind, for me. The mind, the Logos, the reason, the Word made flesh. And what he means to me is the way to live, the truth about reality, and the source of life beyond time.

My friend. He is not only my friend, obviously he is my Savior and my Lord. But in being that, he's not a stern—. He's more like my brother.

... I think sometimes in my own thinking Jesus and God almost become interchangeable, although I'm confident of the fact from Biblical history and what have you that Jesus is the Son of God. But I never see them—I never think of them necessarily as two distinctly different persons.

Only one member could not articulate any particular meaning. Forty-six percent testified that Jesus is held as personal Savior.

Do all religious traditions provide equally valid avenues to God, or is one tradition "better" than others? The latter view, sometimes called *particularism,* rejects the position that any faith is acceptable as long as it helps one get closer to God. The claim that God recognizes only one denomination or tradition is a very narrow form of particularism. A broader form would be represented by the statement that "Christianity is the only acceptable faith, but it doesn't make any difference whether you are Lutheran, Baptist, or Episcopalian."

The narrow form of particularism still survives. Some religious sects and cults thrive because they claim, "Ours is the one way." This view captures some people's individual attention, producing remarkable loyalty and dedication to the "one true faith." Particularism exists even in some mainstream denominations. It was not long ago that Bailey Smith, elected president of the Southern Baptist Convention in 1980, made his now-famous statement: "It's interesting to me at great political battles how you have a Protestant to pray and a Catholic to pray, and then you have a Jew to pray. With all due respect to those dear people, my friend, God Almighty does not hear the prayer of a Jew. For how in the world can God hear the prayer of a man who says that Jesus Christ is not the Messiah? It is blasphemous."[9]

How much particularism exists in the United States Congress? We asked our sample to respond to the statement, There is one religious tradition that is truer than all other traditions. There was dramatic division. Thirty-eight percent firmly agreed; 30 percent firmly disagreed. The others were not willing to take either position. However, there was little evidence of narrow or rigid particularism: only two members claimed that one specific religious tradition within Christianity has a premium on religious truth.

The vast majority who agreed with the statement wanted only to go so far as to say that "Christianity is the truest religion, truer than other world religions like Islam or Hinduism." The disagreers could not say this, claiming instead—as one member put it—that "all the great religions of the world are equally valid ways of knowing God. If I had grown up in India, Hinduism would make more sense than Christianity."

There appears to be much religious tolerance in Congress. Of course, it would be politically dangerous for a member to be narrowly particularistic. If he or she were, it would be best to keep it hidden.

Beliefs about Salvation and Paths to Salvation

It is a condition of human life that we long for something more. As George Thomas puts it, "man is a spiritual being who stands out from and above the rest of nature by his self-awareness, and his capacity for self-transcendence will never permit him to be content with life as it is."[10] A distinguishing mark of all religions—and, from a functional point of view, one of the most important roles religion plays—is to offer "something more," a vision of a fuller life, a completeness, a promise of fulfillment. Van der Leeuw, in his comprehensive *Religion in Essence and Manifestation,* says that "religion is always directed towards salvation, never towards life as it is given; and in this respect all religion, with no exception, is the religion of deliverance."[11]

What is the "more" to life that is promised by religion? In very general terms we can say that there are three basic views of salvation alive in the world.

One view sees salvation in communal and social terms. It is the rebirth of society, the formation of "the kingdom of God on earth." Salvation requires massive social change. "Once all swords have been turned into ploughshares, once social justice has been established, once injustice, oppression, and misery have been banned from the earth and all fears wiped away,"[12] then the promise has been fulfilled. This social kind of salvation has, of course, firm grounding within the Judeo-Christian tradition.

A second view also emphasizes a this-worldly form of salvation, but the transformation is personal, not social. There are elements of this in those Christians who speak of the fruits of faith or the gifts of the spirit. One is changed in some way for the better. Perhaps the most prominent form of salvation-as-personal-transformation occurs in Buddhism. Here we see a description of the human condition as suffering. Suffering is believed to be caused by desire, and suffering ends when desire ceases. Through rigorous efforts to retreat from a life of sensation and pleasure, one ultimately attains Nirvana, a state devoid of suffering, and involving perfect tranquility. This is an example of the axiom that one must give up one's life in order to find it. Buddha was not clear on whether the state of Nirvana continues past mortal life. There is some evidence that in spite of the official teachings of Buddhism, many Buddhists adopt the view that Nirvana continues after the grave.[13]

The third concept of salvation, the one most familiar to Westerners, is personal immortality. The emphasis is not so much on what happens now as on what happens later, after death. It is perhaps the most comforting view and therefore it is psychologically compelling. This is particularly true in cultures like America's, where a premium is placed on individualism. For a person whose identity is premised more on individualism than on community, more on "me" than on "we," the thought that the "me" simply turns to dust is repugnant. The Christian promise of eternal life is attractive. Various branches of Christianity differ on some of the specifics of this form of salvation, such as how long after death resurrection occurs, whether that which survives is only soul or both soul and body, whether one's earthly life is remembered or forgotten, and whether or not one is in the company of loved ones. Though the imagery is rich and diverse on these specific issues, most Christians are united in seeing an afterlife dimension to salvation.

Salvation, we have said, is the concept of the "more" promised by religions. One's belief about salvation is clearly related to two corollary issues: What is the human problem from which salvation delivers us? What is the path to salvation?—that is, how do we move from the problem to the salvation?

At the risk of overwhelming members with a too abstract question, we constructed a diagram that tied the issues together. During the interview each member was handed a copy of the diagram, shown in figure 3-1.

Figure 3-1

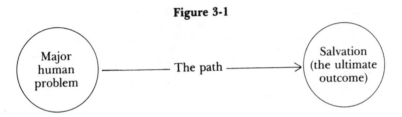

Our introduction to this question went like this:

Religions commonly speak to three issues. They define a major human problem or limitation, they promise some ultimate outcome (often called salvation) and a path that leads from the problem to this ultimate outcome. What is the human problem your religion deals with? What is the ultimate outcome? What is salvation? And what is the path to salvation? How does one get there?

In some interviews there followed the sound of shifting feet, periods of silence, and deeply indrawn breaths. These are not matters of daily reflection. In Congress, in the midst of practical life, such a broad-ranging theoretical question constituted a bit of a shock. In time, however, each was able to articulate a response. Some treated the three issues as individual pieces, seemingly not seeing the logical interconnection among them.

Others saw the integration and wove together a united response. (See table 3-10.)

Table 3-10

Statement	Percentage Who Gave This Response
What is the *human problem* your religion deals with?	
Estrangement from God	20
Lack of meaning, purpose, direction in individual lives	50
Lack of human community, need for guidance on how to live corporate life	15
Human suffering, misery	2
Other	12
What is the *path to salvation?* How does one get there?*	
Faith—something God does (e.g., a gift from God, forgiveness, the gift of grace freely given)	37
Works—something people do to "earn" salvation	
Doing good—love, compassion, caring	50
Living virtuously—avoiding evil, pursuing virtue	39
Predestination	3
Discover God's plan for my life	4
Don't know	6
What is the ultimate outcome? What is *salvation?**	
Sin overcome	12
Reconciliation with God	13
New social order	21
Personal transformation in this life (more joy, fulfillment, meaning, etc.)	38
Life after death; personal immortality	51
Life after death; reincarnation	3
Term not meaningful, not sure	12
Other	3

*Percentages sum to more than 100 percent because some members gave more than one response.

Half of the responses to the human-problem question say that some needed quality is lacking in individual life. Twenty percent use traditional theological terms about sin and estrangement. Fifteen percent believe the problem is more social and corporate; they point out the lack of community among people.

Salvation is most frequently identified as personal immortality. Several members mentioned reincarnation (being reborn after death into another earthly life), a view common to Eastern religions. This is one of only a few places in the interview where Eastern concepts were in evidence.

In answers to the path-to-salvation question, we see evidence of a theological split—the split between "faith" and "works." Many Protestant traditions teach that salvation is a gift from God, something unearned. A gift cannot be earned—if it is, then it becomes a wage and loses its gift status. God does the saving; people don't save themselves through any effort of their own. It is heresy in many Protestant traditions to claim that one can be saved through one's actions. Nonetheless, the two predominant categories of congressional response are of the works variety. One is saved through efforts to do good or saved through efforts to avoid vice and seek virtue.

The predominance of these categories reflects the general culture. For example, in a massive, national study of Lutherans conducted by Search Institute staff in 1970, it was found that a majority of Lutherans professed a works orientation to salvation[14]—this in the face of official Lutheran doctrine which clearly articulates a faith orientation. Why do people resist the gift-from-God message? It may be because American society is a works society. We are socialized from many quarters to believe that we are what we do or that we get what we earn. Our material life outcomes depend not on gifts freely given, but on what we merit. Effort equals rewards. We are an achieving society. It becomes very difficult, given the power and constant presence of achievement-oriented cultural symbols and social messages, to believe that anything is truly free.

The percentages of the path-to-salvation answers add up to more than 100 percent because some members gave two paths. When this happened, it was usually because he or she referred to both types of works—"doing good" and "living virtuously." Only 3 percent claimed a belief in predestination, which refers to the doctrine that God decides ahead of time to save some and damn others.

Members of Congress, more than half the time, put together their three responses (problem, path, outcome) in predictable packages. Figure 3-2 shows the three most common packages of

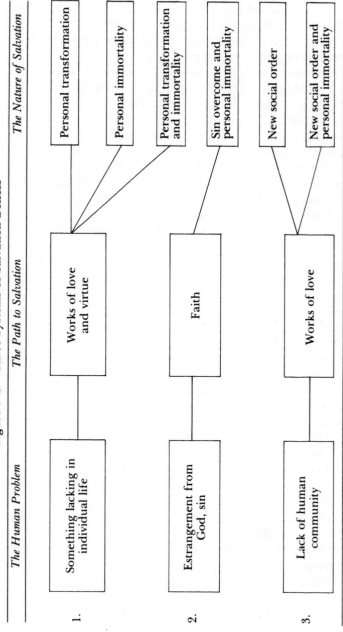

Figure 3-2. Three Systems of Salvation Beliefs

	The Human Problem	The Path to Salvation	The Nature of Salvation
1.	Something lacking in individual life	Works of love and virtue	Personal transformation Personal immortality Personal transformation and immortality
2.	Estrangement from God, sin	Faith	Sin overcome and personal immortality
3.	Lack of human community	Works of love	New social order New social order and personal immortality

beliefs about salvation. About 60 percent of our sample fit into one of these three systems. System 1 represents about 30 percent of our total sample. The problem is expressed in human or psychological terms; the path is a works orientation with emphasis on both varieties—doing good and living virtuously—and salvation is construed as personal transformation in this life, or personal immortality, or both.

System 2 represents about 20 percent of our sample. The problem is couched in theological terms: it is sin, or our severed relationship with God, that plagues us. If the problem is understood in this way, then the path becomes one of faith, of accepting God's forgiveness. Salvation is defined as sin overcome and personal immortality.

Systems 1 and 2 are different versions of an individualism motif—both state the problem in individual terms, and salvation is an individual outcome. System 3 (10 percent) parts company with them on both counts. It defines the problem as communal and describes the outcome also as at least partly communal.

Beliefs about Last Things

For some people salvation and eschatology overlap. In the previous section we saw that some people define salvation as life after death. Eschatology usually covers a range of topics: How and when does resurrection occur? Is it only the soul that is immortal? What is the final judgment process like? How many life-after-death options are there? (How many different places can God send us?) What is life after death like? (What happens? What do people do?) We regret that the interview did not allow time to probe deeply this rich and varied terrain.[15] We did, however, pursue several general questions about life after death. (See table 3-11.)

We opened the discussion by asking, "Is there life after death?" For those favorable to the concept we asked whether life after death included heaven, or hell, or both, and whether individuality is lost or preserved in the hereafter. A strong majority believe that life after death occurs. Many understand life after death in relatively traditional terms of heaven and hell. Only 5 percent affirm heaven but reject belief in hell. Of

Table 3-11

Statement	Percentage Who Gave This Response
Is there life after death?	
Yes	81
Not sure	10
No	9
Conception of life after death (for those saying "yes" above)	
Both heaven and hell exist	56
Heaven exists, but not hell	5
There is reward and punishment after death but not comfortable with terms *heaven* and *hell*	4
Reincarnation	3
Not sure how to describe it but believe in life after death	13
In heaven, is individuality lost or preserved?	
Individuality preserved	51
Individuality lost	23
Don't know	26

those who say they accept the concept of heaven, about one-half assert that individuality will be preserved, and about one-quarter believe individuality will be lost. The view that individuality will be lost goes hand in hand with other beliefs which reflect an emphasis more on community than on individuality.

Beliefs about People and Society

One's views of people and society reflect or are shaped by the affirmation of Religious Reality. We selected three people-and-society issues for inclusion in the interview: human nature, social causation, and social change. We focused on these because they provide a bridge between one's religious views and one's political ideology. We will explore here how the three are tied to one's beliefs about Religious Reality.

The identity of the forces that shape human nature is an issue debated in both religious and political circles. For both it is a pivotal issue. From a religious point of view one's view of human nature is closely tied to how one understands God, salvation, and ethics. In the political domain one's view of human nature influences one's conception of how society should be structured and governed.

We asked members to say how true each of these six statements about human nature are:

- People are predominantly evil and sinful.
- People are predominantly good.
- People are selfish and competitive.
- People are loving and cooperative.
- People are perfectible, given the right social conditions.
- People are not perfectible. There are no social conditions that can overcome human evil.

These six images can be collapsed into three dimensions of human nature (shown in figure 3-3, along with the distribution of members' answers). Overall, Congress inclines toward a positive view of human nature. The opinion is certainly not unanimous that, for example, people are more good than evil, but the emphasis is in that direction. Our sample leans noticeably toward belief in human perfectibility.

Another social concept at the heart of both religious and political ideology is causation: What is most responsible for determining human behavior? Do people choose their actions through an exercise of free will? Do we act because of the motives and values we have been socialized to adopt? Are we simply the products of our particular social environment, governed by the economic and political realities of our location in society? Or does God rule lives, cutting through our individual and social circumstances to accomplish some purpose or to steer us in some particular direction? These are not simple or mutually exclusive categories. Most of us probably adopt some kind of compromise position. Nonetheless, each person has a general emphasis or perspective. Table 3-12 shows how members of Congress responded.

We asked each member to consider the relative importance of eight factors for determining what happens in people's lives, for creating their fortunes and misfortunes. God is the highest-ranked causal factor. It may be that the estimate of God's influence was inflated by the interview itself. After all, we were talking about religion, and the concept of God may have become

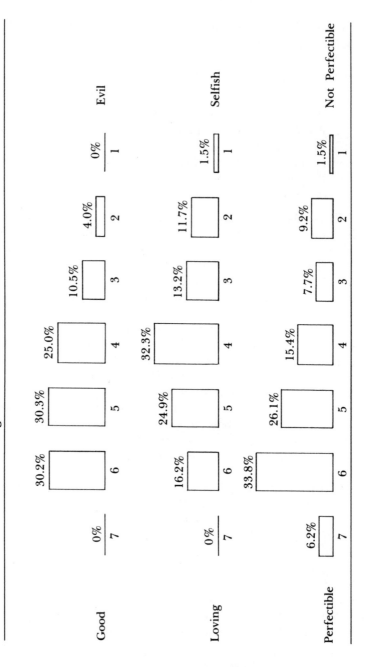

Figure 3-3. Views of Human Nature

more prominent in members' minds than it normally is. Satan, or some evil force, takes last place in influence. Only 13 percent attribute any major significance to the presence of Satan or some evil force in the world; 64 percent attribute no importance at all to Satan.

Table 3-12

Statement: How much do each of the following eight factors have to do with determining what happens in people's lives?	Average on Seven-point Scale from Not Important (1) to Extremely Important (7)
God	5.06
The kind of environment one grew up in	4.89
One's values and motives	4.80
Free will	4.51
The social system—its economic and political arrangements	4.46
One's abilities and skills	4.13
One's inherited traits and capacities	3.88
Satan or some evil force	2.83

The remaining six factors (table 3-12) are of two types. Four are statements about individual characteristics (values, free will, abilities, traits), and two are statements about the social context in which one lives (environment, political and economic arrangements). Neither the individualistic nor the social context (systemic) explanation for human behavior predominates.

How members view the causes of social problems is tied to their views of social change. To explore the latter we asked this question:

There are two common positions on the best way to approach social problems (for example, poverty, crime, violence). One approach says the best way to address these problems is by transforming the hearts of individuals. The other calls for transforming social institutions and structures. Which one is closest to your position?

A hearts approach conceives of social change from the bottom up. It implies that the solution to social problems lies in changing the attitudes and values of the American public. The other approach to social change is a "top-down" theory. Here, social problems are confronted by changing the social structures which are seen to constrain or limit people. The poor break out of poverty by being on the receiving end of economic or educational changes. Tax relief for those with low incomes is one such approach. Improving the educational environment in inner-city schools is another. As the numbers in table 3-13 indicate, Congress leans toward a hearts approach to social change.

Table 3-13

Statement	Percentage Who Gave This Response
Transform hearts	39
Emphasize transformation of hearts but pay attention also to transforming system	19
Transform both heart and system	19
Emphasize transformation of system but pay attention also to transforming hearts	16
Transform system	7

Positions on this hearts-versus-system question are tied to views of both social causation and human nature. Those who lean toward changing the social system tend to see human behavior caused by social and economic forces and tend to be generous on the human-nature question. Those who seek social change via a hearts approach tend to see human life shaped more by individualistic factors like free will, values, and motives, and have a less positive opinion of human nature.

These two different combinations of beliefs about people and society are also tied to God-images. Those with a more individualistic approach to social causation and social change view God in very personal terms, adopting many of the images associated with the "Companion God" discussed at the start of this chapter. Those who take a more systemic approach to social causation and social change are more likely to image God in communal and abstract ways.

Beliefs about Values, Ethical Principles, and Responsibilities

Religion plays many roles in a person's life. It offers perspective and meaning. It provides a framework for understanding past, present, and future. As important as any of these functions is the role it plays as action-guide, steering behavior in certain directions. That is, religion helps people deal with the question, How should I lead my life? Each of us has to make choices about what is important, what is desirable, what is good, and what is evil. These are questions of values. They are subjective judgments, and we all make them whether we recognize it or not. Religion brings to the issue of values a certain authority. It says that some value-orientations are better than others and justifies these claims on an understanding of the nature and purpose of Religious Reality.[16]

In reviewing the moral prescriptions of many religions—both within the Judeo-Christian framework and outside it—we find four value systems consistently advocated. Most religions consider all four, though the emphases vary. The four are as follows:

Self-restraint. The emphasis in this value system is on refraining from particular behaviors. A self-restraint approach to values tends to encourage constraint in areas like sexuality, drugs, language, and interpersonal relationships. The desired direction is toward purity of thought and action, replacing vice with virtue.

Home, family, and nation. A second common value-orientation advocates the primacy of home, family, and nation. It is a good-citizenship orientation that urges one to take responsibility for protecting and promoting the society at large and the foundational units on which it is organized. It is rendering unto Caesar the things that are Caesar's. This orientation tends more toward social stability than toward social change.

Love. The great religions of the world—Buddhism, Hinduism, Islam, Judaism, Christianity—give significant attention to how persons should relate to others. All of these prescribe a charitable, merciful, compassionate attitude. The message is that narcissism and selfishness must be replaced with concern for others. In short, this is an ethic of love, a prominent theme in the New Testament.

Social justice. Like a love-orientation a social justice approach seeks to improve the human condition. In a love approach the method is face to face. In a social-justice approach the method is on changing the social conditions that create pain and misfortune for individuals. People define justice differently. Some see justice as meaning equal opportunity for all, and some think it means equal outcomes for all. In either case there is the conviction that at least part of an individual's pain is caused by "the system"—abuses of power, unequal educational or job opportunities, inequitable access to money and means of procuring money. A social-justice orientation seeks social or environmental change as a way to improve the lot of individuals.

We asked members, "What do your religious beliefs and convictions tell you about how you should lead your life? What should you seek to be or do? Try to give as many words or phrases as possible." We placed each comment in one of the four value-orientation categories. Our sample of eighty members produced a total of 162 codeable responses to this question. (Some people gave two answers to the question and a few gave three.) One hundred and forty-nine of these fit into one or the other of the four value-orientations. The distribution is remarkably even among the four.

Self-Restraint Orientation Responses (27 Percent)

Examples of response:

God will judge me someday on how I've led my life. If I've been good, kept his commandments, and tried my best to stay in line, then he will take me to heaven.

This country is going downhill because so many want pleasure for themselves. The Roman Empire collapsed because people got too loose in their morals. We've got to have rules to guide our conduct, or we, too, will collapse.

Home/Family/Nation Orientation Responses (24 Percent)

Examples of response:

The family is at the core of both the Bible and American society. I feel a heavy responsibility for bringing the family back into the American way of life.

I feel a special calling to serve my country. I'm in political life because God wants me here.

Love Orientation Responses (24 Percent)

Examples of response:

I believe I should act in the image of Christ, trying to be as kind and considerate and loving as I can to other people.

I think God demands goodness and love and commitment to this world apart from any rewards. And that's what makes Christianity tough—because humanity wants reward. Love your fellow man because it's right, not because it will get you to heaven.

Social Justice Orientation Responses (26 Percent)

Examples of response:

I must help create a more just society, one where everyone has a fair chance to make it.

This heaven stuff is a crutch for a lot of people. What matters is making this a better world. God wants us to jump in and get our hands dirty, helping overcome the poverty and hunger and disease that cripple so many people.

More than a third of the interviewees were "pure types" on this question, all of their value statements fitting into a single category. The rest mentioned value statements that fit into two or more categories, giving evidence of a broader view of the effect that religious belief should have on life. The three most common mixtures were self-restraint combined with home/family/nation; self-restraint combined with love; and love combined with social justice.

In later chapters we will see that where a member is located on these four values is one of the most telling indicators of how he or she votes on important legislative issues.

The Myth in Focus

> *Myth Number One:* The U.S. Congress is a hotbed of secular humanism, agnosticism, and atheism.

It is no secret among those who live in the spotlight of public attention that negative comment—criticism, allegations of wrongdoing, and unfavorable labels, whether grounded in fact or not—easily attracts the attention of the press and the public.

Tim LaHaye, in *The Battle for the Mind*, says:

There can be no question that the humanists control our government, and have for many years. . . . Those 537 people [he includes the President and Vice-President] who control our national destiny represent sufficient humanistic philosophy or lack of true Christian consensus to have brought us to the threshold of fulfilling the humanist dreams of a secular, amoral society.[17]

Claims of this kind have stimulated a national debate on the extent and impact of the so-called humanist explosion. The weight of the evidence reported in this chapter suggests that the LaHaye statement is wide of the mark. We do not contend that Congress is ready for nomination to sainthood; on the other hand, our findings about Congress do not seem to support the LaHaye denunciation. A summary of some of the major discoveries about the religious beliefs of Congress outlined earlier in this chapter may make the point clear.

1. Nearly all members of Congress affirm a belief in God. Nearly all are able to talk with understanding and coherence about their convictions in seven major categories of religious belief.
2. The beliefs of Congress outline a good-sized area of consensus of belief. The majority of people in Congress agree that:

a) There is a Religious Reality, a being or force called God.
b) God is both transcendent and immanent.
c) God is involved in the course of history.
d) Scripture is more than myth and allegory; God was involved in its development, though Scripture may not be perfectly accurate in every detail.
e) The church is a constructive means for coming to know God.
f) Jesus was both divine and human.
g) There is life after death, and in that life individuality is preserved.
h) Both heaven and hell exist.
i) People tend more toward good than toward evil, and they are perfectible, given the right conditions.

The evidence is strong that the majority of Congress is a believing Congress. The *secular humanist* epithet used by LaHaye and others who speak for the conservative political movement known as the New Christian Right does not even approach accuracy except perhaps as applied to a small proportion of members of Congress. Yet the charge is leveled against large segments of Congress, sometimes even at Congress as a whole.

Who are the opposition? They are those whose politically liberal votes favor programs and policies that the New Christian Right considers "wrong." One of the saddest things about this war of words is that some of those against whom the epithet is most vigorously used are also among those most deeply committed to their religious faith. Whatever the differences from their New Christian Right critics, they are not primarily differences in degree of religious commitment.

4. How Important Is Religion to Members of Congress?

IN THE preceding chapter we dealt principally with the religious beliefs, concepts, attitudes, and values of members of Congress. But it is also important to gather information about the religious behaviors and experiences of such a group to see whether the concepts they articulate are matched by experience and action. We can envision skeptics saying, "Talk is cheap. What do members of Congress *do* that qualifies them to be considered religious?"

Partly in an effort to test the congruence or variance with the beliefs, attitudes, and values expressed in the early part of the interview, and partly in order to enlarge the total religious portrait, we asked members of Congress some questions about several common indicators of religious involvement. Two of the usual ways in which the average citizen makes informal judgments about others' religious involvement is by observing their religion-related behavior and by hearing the kinds of religion-related experiences they report. Our interview questions focused on both public and private religious behavior, on the kinds of specific religious experiences members reported having had, and on their own estimate of the importance of religion in their lives.

Religious Behavior: Public

Ninety percent of our sample claim affiliation with a specific church or synagogue. (See table 4-1.) Another 4 percent identify with a religious tradition (e.g., Episcopalian, Lutheran) but are not currently on the membership roster of any particular congregation. The remaining 6 percent do not identify with any specific religious tradition, either by heritage or by membership.

Table 4-1

Statement	Percentage Who Gave This Response
Are you currently a member of a church or synagogue?	
Yes	90
No	10
How often do you attend worship services?	
More than once a week	3
Weekly	29
One to three times a month	42
Less than once a month	26

Almost one-third attend church services at least once a week, and three-fourths attend at least once a month. Many pointed out that being in Congress severely interferes with church attendance. There are the frequent treks to the home state or district on weekends, with speaking dates and obligatory appearances scheduled, and return-to-Washington flights on Sunday. In campaign years candidates are often out shaking hands at the local supermarket on Sunday mornings. Some younger members of Congress remarked that they had not had time yet to locate a Washington-area church or synagogue with which to affiliate. However, given all the interferences named, it is noteworthy that attendance is as high as it is.

We asked members to describe "the kinds of leadership roles you have taken in a church or synagogue." A remarkable 80 percent could cite at least one such activity. The percentages of our sample who have engaged in each of six church leadership roles are shown in table 4-2.

It is natural to assume that persons elected to Congress have a history as community leaders. Church leadership appears often to have been a part of that community involvement.

In addition to inquiring about their history in church leadership, we asked about their current religious participation. We expected that, given extreme demands on members' time, their

Table 4-2

Role	Percentage Who Gave This Response
Deacon, elder, or church council member	42
Sunday school teacher	36
Preached occasionally	18
Member or director of church choir	14
Led Bible studies	6
Worker with youth	3

current activity might be quite low. We were surprised to find as many of them active as the figures in table 4-3 indicate.

Few members, then, have rejected institutionalized religion. Although not many are intensely active during their years in Congress, most have a history of church leadership and maintain at least a moderate level of participation while serving in Congress.

Table 4-3

Degree of Church Activity	Percentage Who Fit This Classification
Extremely active: Major leadership position, highly visible in church or synagogue	5
Quite active: Weekly attendance plus involvement in weekday activities	10
Somewhat active: Attendance three or four times per month	27
Slightly active: Visible at church or synagogue once or twice a month for worship or other activity	41
Not active: Participation rare or nonexistent	16

Religious Behavior: Private

Prayer is apparently a frequent occurrence among members. (See table 4-4.) Almost half pray once a day or more. Only 15 percent say they infrequently or never pray. Scripture reading does not fare so well. The frequency of reading Scripture is almost the reverse of the reported frequency of prayer. Forty-six percent read Scripture only occasionally or never.

Table 4-4

Statement	Percentage Who Gave This Response
How often, if at all, do you pray?	
Daily or more often	48
Weekly or more often, but not daily	26
Several times a month	12
Occasionally	10
Never	5
How often, if at all, do you read Scripture?	
Daily or more often	5
Weekly or more often, but not daily	32
Several times a month	16
Occasionally	33
Never	13

We said earlier that one of the inevitable questions raised about this study is that members' self-reported beliefs and behaviors were likely to be inflated for political reasons, thereby raising a question about the validity of our findings. We claimed in chapter 1 that we thought this social-desirability problem was not extreme. The Scripture-reading finding lends credence to that claim. Although it would have been easy to inflate one's answer on this question, members apparently did not.

Religious Experience

Religion for many people is a mostly cognitive activity. When an emotional religious experience occurs, it is usually memorable. We asked congressional interviewees about seven kinds of religious experience that have emotional overtones. Their responses, given in the order in which the questions were asked, are shown in table 4-5.

Two figures that may surprise readers are the large numbers reporting the experiences of "specific answer to prayer" and "feeling God's presence."

Table 4-5

Statement	Yes	Not Sure	No
God speaking to me	22	5	74
Feeling God's presence	78	3	18
Feeling one with God	46	5	49
Feeling united with the universe	22	11	67
Have had a born-again experience	30	1	69
Speaking in tongues	3	0	97
Specific answer to prayer	65	10	25

Note: Percentages rounded to nearest whole number.

"Feeling one with God" and "feeling united with the universe" are often called mystical experiences. The former is a distinctly Judeo-Christian version of mysticism. The latter is more common in Eastern religions, yet almost a quarter of members report experiencing it.

The born-again question was phrased like this: Have you had a born-again experience in which Jesus entered your life? This, of course, is a distinguishing characteristic of those who call themselves evangelical Christians. Nearly one member in three claims such an experience. Most of them describe it as a gradual process rather than a sudden experience.

Do members of Congress who report several religious experiences differ in other religious ways from those who report none? Not surprisingly, those who have had a number of religious experiences tend to place more importance on religion, engage more often in religious behaviors like prayer and church attendance, and describe God in highly personal terms. We cannot tell whether such experiences come more readily to those who consider religion central to their lives or whether the experiences had the effect of increasing the centrality of religion in the person's life. Both may be true.

Importance of Religion

The vast majority of members can articulate a set of religious beliefs about God, salvation, eschatology, and ethical guidelines. Are these utterances mere words, peripheral to the rest of life, or are they an important part of the lives of members of Congress? In order to assess not only how important religion is to the interviewee now, but how this importance has changed throughout one's life cycle, we devised a *religious lifeline.*[2] Each member was asked to draw on a form like the one in figure 4-1 a line depicting religious import since age fifteen.

Figure 4-1

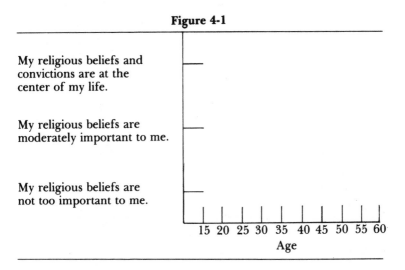

Indications of the current importance of religion to all eighty interviewees are summarized in figure 4-2. The preponderant choice was on the high side of "moderately important," where 37 percent placed themselves. Another third said that religion was at the center of their lives. Overall, most members said that religion is important to them.

Those who take a jaundiced view of Congress might well charge that this method makes a self-inflated rating not only easy but likely. We had a similar concern. As a way of checking the legitimacy of these self-reports, we asked the interview coders to estimate the importance of religion to each interviewee. The coders assigned this rating on a seven-point religion-is-central to religion-is-peripheral continuum. They made this assignment immediately *after* listening to a member's taped interview and *before* seeing a member's lifeline. Each of the coders has

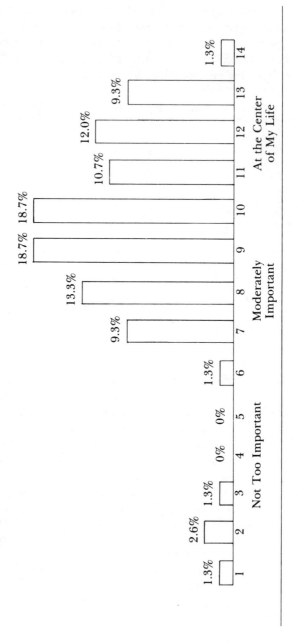

Figure 4-2. Distribution of Current Importance of Religion

had extensive experience in "listening between the lines," paying attention to how things are said as much as to what is said. Though words can deceive, the between-the-lines cues—the feeling tone, the emphases, the nuances—are nearly impossible to fake across an entire thirty-minute interview. We found that the coders' ratings of religious importance correlated strongly with members' self-assessments of religious importance, suggesting that the high level of centrality members attached to their religious beliefs is real and meaningful.[3]

There are nearly as many different lifelines as there are members in our sample. There are some common types, however, as presented in figure 4-3. In the diagrams we spotted some interesting dynamics. Most members experience some increase in the importance assigned to religion starting at about age thirty. In some cases the increase is slow and gradual; in a few cases it is dramatic. Importance, if it declines, does so in the twenties, during the time of college, military service, and initiating a career. For most of the declines there is a rebound. When we combine the sharp U-shape type with the shallow U-shape, we see that the decline-and-rebound pattern has been experienced by about a third of our sample. Something seems to occur in one's thirties that brings about a religious reawakening. Recent work in adult stages of development suggests that the thirties are a time for reevaluation of one's life, a time to put things in perspective. Apparently, for many members this effort to seek perspective included a reaffirmation of religion.

Does Washington Strengthen or Inhibit Religious Faith?

There is no doubt that the experience of serving in Congress radically alters the shape of a person's life. Members are surrounded with power and privilege of a style and magnitude many have never experienced before. They are in demand, both socially and politically. They are surrounded by staffs who swiftly and competently do their bidding, shield them from unwanted interruptions, and handle complex details on their behalf. But, for all the power and privilege gained, members pay a high price in terms of stress. Families are uprooted; life is lived in a fish bowl; constituents and colleagues are there to watch every move; one feels always "on stage," always being

Figure 4-3. Religious Importance: Six Most Common Types of Lifelines

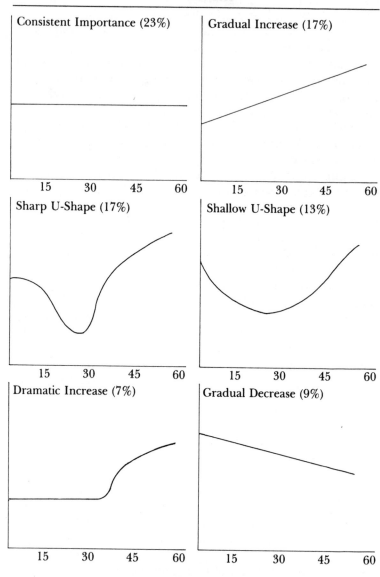

Note: These graphs are presented only to illustrate the variety in shape of line drawn by the members of Congress. The location of the line does not represent the average location of lifelines drawn in the congressional interview.

careful to put the best foot forward. All of this would seem enough to alter a person's view of the world, and perhaps to have some effect on one's religious views as well.

To assess what effect the pressures of life in Washington have on one's religious inclination, we looked again at the religious lifeline drawn by each member. For each member we compared the point on the line representing current religious importance with the point on the line when he or she first entered Congress. For only 3 percent did importance decline during the period of service in Congress. For almost half it increased.

Three Ways of Being Religious

Almost universally, the first question asked of the writers when the name of this study was offered and the study described was, "Is there any religion on Capitol Hill?" The universal interest expressed in the question confirmed our intention to go deeper than the "importance" question to give those who ask that question a relatively simple but accurate response. What one person describes as important could look very superficial to someone else. To some people religion merits the label *important* only when it encompasses all of life, being visible in how one thinks, speaks, feels, and acts. To others religion that touches only the intellect can be deemed important and vital. Accordingly, to say that most members of Congress perceive religion to be important in their lives is not enough. We looked deeper in an attempt to establish how vital and central religion really is for members of Congress.

There are general ways in which religion is experienced. These differ mainly in how much of one's life it touches. We call these three *religion as total commitment, religion as moderate commitment,* and *religion as casual commitment.* They differ not by the content of religious belief but by the way one's religious ideas and images—regardless of what they are—operate in one's life. We used several sources of information to place members in one of these three named categories. These sources include:

1. The emphasis and certainty of statement of religious beliefs. When coding the content of beliefs about God, Scrip-

ture, human nature, etc., the coders also recorded how emphatically or certainly stated each belief statement was.

2. The clarity with which members could say how their religious beliefs had changed or affected their life.

3. Frequency of religious behavior (e.g., prayer, Scripture reading).

4. Frequency and intensity of religious experiences.

5. Coder ratings. Each interview coder rated each interview on a number of religious dynamics. After listening to what was said and how it was said, each coder estimated the degree to which each member's religion was vital, examined, concrete, "engaging the whole person," and peripheral. These ratings were not blind guesses. Coders working independently of each other had a high degree of correspondence when rating the same interviewees.[4]

All of these units of information from each congressional interview were summed and analyzed to see how members of Congress divided themselves into the three categories we now describe.[5]

Religion as Total Commitment

Religion as total commitment means that religious faith has taken over one's life. It goes much beyond professing a set of beliefs. Religion becomes a way of seeing life and acting in it. But it also has an emotional or experiential component—it is religion that is felt. And it is visible on the plane of action. It informs decisions, guides behavior, and colors one's style of relating to others. Religion becomes the mainspring, the inner dynamic which organizes, interprets, and guides all of life. Religion as total commitment is like being in love—one's whole life has been grasped, changed, and altered. We found that 24 percent of Congress can properly be described as experiencing a religion of total commitment.

Religion as Moderate Commitment

To a middle-distance observer the religious activity of the moderately committed may not look much different from that of the totally committed. It is a form of religious commitment prevalent in American churches. It is the form of commitment of the moderately active, moderately involved churchgoer who does most of the right things, who occasionally ponders the meaning of life, who can, if asked, articulate his or her religious ideas, and who occasionally calls on his or her religion for solace or direction. But in describing this form of religious experience, we find that we are continually qualifying—it is *somewhat* experiential, *somewhat* certain, *somewhat* practiced, *modestly* clear about values and ethics, *sometimes* influencing decisions. There seems to be a lid on this religion; it shows many of the signs of a life-encompassing faith, but it also holds something back. The activity is metered, controlled, exercised in measured amounts. There is reluctance about totally giving in to it, as if one feared that all control would be lost in allowing oneself to be firmly grasped by Religious Reality. The religious expression is faithful, but it lacks passion. It is affirmed, but compartmentalized. One can imagine someone with this form of commitment designating one portion of life as religious and other portions as nonreligious. Religion as moderate commitment may be quite common among males. In our culture men are socialized to be in control, in charge. Total commitment demands a willingness to give up control to God. A fear of surrendering control may inhibit men from moving beyond religion as moderation. We discovered that about half (49 percent) of Congress belongs to this category.

Religion as Casual Commitment

At the other extreme is another religious experience which is only "in the head." James Dittes, a psychologist of religion at Yale, gives a penetrating description of this way of being religious. He says that for this type, religion

is a casual attitude, acquired mindlessly and passionlessly, along with other conventions and habits, like brushing one's teeth or saying "How do you do?" It represents and derives from solidarity with a social group, but . . . cannot possibly generate or enhance such solidarity, for it neither attracts nor generates passions or energies, becomes visible or articulate only when some outside energy calls it forth, such as that of a survey researcher asking "Do you believe . . . ?" But the belief has no salience, no power. It bears no relationship to the person's basic energies or yearnings.... It claims no energies. It simply lies there, dormant, with a multitude of companions, any one of which can be recalled momentarily to consciousness and conversation by suitable external stimulus.[6]

About a quarter (24 percent) of our sample fell into this category.

Half of our sample falls into the moderate-commitment category, and about a quarter each into the total-commitment and casual-commitment categories. By combining the moderate-commitment and total-commitment categories, we can say that three-quarters of the members of the U.S. Congress are genuinely religious, to the point where religion is a definite influence on their thoughts and actions, an integral part of their lives.

Reasons for Silence About Religion in Congress

The information in this chapter only serves to reinforce the conclusion, first drawn in chapter 3, that Congress is populated with a substantial number of people to whom religion matters. The evidence confirms our conviction that to depict Congress as a hotbed of secular humanism is seriously in error.

It is curious that this understanding of the religious nature of Congress has not previously come to light. There are probably several reasons for the silence. One is the preference of some members, shared by many other citizens, not to reveal their religous sentiments publicly. In part their motivation may be fear that to do so would offend some voters. The silence may also be due in part to the relative lack of interest in religion on the part of social scientists, mentioned in chapter 1, with the result that the presence or influence of religious belief on Congress has simply not been seriously studied.

Another important factor contributing to our ignorance of religion on Capitol Hill may be the particular kind of mental filter common among those who serve as our major source of information about Congress—the national press. A recent survey of 240 top journalists and broadcasters working with some of the most prominent of the media outlets (e.g., *New York Times, Washington Post, Time, Newsweek,* CBS, NBC, and ABC) suggests that "a predominant characteristic of the media elite is its secular outlook. Exactly 50 percent eschew any religious affiliation. . . . Only 8 percent go to church or synagogue weekly, and 86 percent seldom or never attend religious services."[7] The national press, then, may not be interested in reporting on religion on Capitol Hill, or perhaps the reporters and commentators are unable to recognize religious influence when they see it. In either case, it seems possible that the press is involved in creating the impression that religion is not an important part of life for members of Congress.

5. Is Congress as Religious as the American Public?

Myth Number Two: Members of Congress are
less religious than the people they serve.

AMERICAN citizens, if polled, would probably say that national political leaders are less religious than the people they serve. We know of no poll actually done on this issue, but the perception seems to be widespread. Some religious leaders boldly state it as a fact. Jerry Falwell, a principal figure in the Moral Majority movement, devotes a good deal of his writing and speaking energy to claiming that the spiritual dimension which he declares is alive among America's people is dead among national decision makers. The public, he says, is still in tune with spiritual principles but has been "lax in voting in and out of office the right and wrong people."[1] What we face now, says Falwell, is a crisis in leadership:

Why do we have so few good leaders? Why is it that political and judicial decisions are made that horrify America? You will find that when society begins to fall apart spiritually, what we find missing is the mighty man, that man who is willing, with courage and confidence, to stand up for that which is right. We are hard-pressed to find today that man in a governmental position, that man of war, that judge, that prophet, that preacher who is willing to call sin by its right name. . . . We have few we can look to and say, "Here is an example of godliness in leadership." Instead we find confusion and selfishness, which is destroying the very basis of our society.[2]

Falwell wants "men of God." Our data indicate that a goodly number of men of God are already in Congress. Presumably, what he is asking for is men of God who stand up for positions espoused by the Moral Majority. Nonetheless, his pronouncements have fed a national perception that Congress does not adequately represent the religious values and interests of the American people.

The belief that political leaders are less religious than the public has recently been reinforced by a widely read study on America's values called *The Connecticut Mutual Life Report on American Values in the '80s: The Impact of Belief.*[3] Based on a survey of beliefs held by a national sample and on surveys of leaders in the areas of religion, the military, business, voluntary associations, education, news, medicine, science, and government, the report concludes that "American leaders are out of tune with the public which they are presumed to represent."[4] Government leaders were found to be lower than the public on all measures of religion. Also, compared to other groups of leaders they were consistently at the low end of religious interest and involvement. What was not made clear was that the government officials in the study *were not members of Congress* but federal bureaucrats. Only the most discriminating readers of the study would be aware of this. The inference most people would make upon hearing about the Connecticut Mutual study is that members of Congress are not particularly religious, since the term *government official* is taken by many to mean Congress.

Perhaps this national perception of a less religious Congress is fed by a syllogistic reasoning process that goes like this: (1) Religion is necessary for developing morality; (2) Many members of Congress are dishonest and out for their own benefit; (3) Therefore, members of Congress do not take religion seriously.

Part 1 in this syllogism is an ancient axiom. We don't know who first said it, but it is now firmly entrenched in the American consciousness. It is what drives young parents back to churches, searching for a religious context that will help them impart moral principles to their children. The truth of proposition 1, however, is debatable.

Proposition 2 is widely believed. Most people's exposure to Congress is not personal. It is through the media that we learn about Congress, and the media tend to make a bigger deal of

sinners than of saints. When the public is asked what characteristic they most want in leaders, their first reply is likely to be
honesty. Not competence, or intelligence, but honesty. And
when asked how much confidence they have in Congress, they
turn thumbs down, viewing Congress, in the aggregate, as
about as trustworthy as the proverbial used car salesman.[5] It has
become a conversational commonplace to attribute a lack of
morality to Congress. Thus, part 3 of the syllogism becomes a
truth for many people.

The perception that members do not represent the people—
on religious or on moral and ethical positions—has some un-
pleasant implications. There is no doubt that Americans feel
disillusionment with the political process. They show this alienation by staying away from the voting booth in numbers that
appear to be increasing. This alienation must in part reflect the
feeling that Congress and other people who run our country
are out of step with their constituencies. The question, then,
about whether Congress is *really* in tune with the people on a
matter like religion is more than an intellectual exercise. The
answer has broad social and political implications.

Comparing Congress and the Public

In order to compare the religious sentiments of Congress
with those of the American public, we combed through recent
Gallup polls for information on the public. Gallup chooses a
national, random sample for each of these polls. Accordingly,
Gallup can claim that what is found to be true for the random
sample is true for the public at large. It must be kept in mind
that any attempt to compare Congress and the public is fraught
with difficulties. Our interview was done at the place of work,
amid the hustle and bustle of the day's business. Gallup's interviews are done in the privacy of the home. Our interview was
longer and more intense than the typical Gallup poll. On those
religious subjects where we and Gallup overlap, our interview
questions were rarely worded exactly like Gallup's. Precisely
how these kinds of differences bias the comparison is not
known. Given this ambiguity, conclusions must be made cau-
tiously.[6] However, comparisons are worth making.

There are four religious belief areas and seven behavior and experience areas on which Gallup's data and our interview overlap. The four belief issues presented in table 5-1 all represent orthodox Christian beliefs. Both the public and Congress overwhelmingly report that God exists, Jesus is divine, Scripture is the Word of God, and life after death occurs. The only graphic discrepancy is the public's lesser acceptance of the belief that Jesus Christ is both divine and human.

A slightly higher percentage of the public than of members of Congress affirms that Jesus Christ is divine. However, on the question of Jesus being both divine and human—one of the standard teachings of all major Christian churches—the percentage of the public able to accept the statement drops off dramatically. In Congress almost all of those who affirmed Jesus' divine nature also affirmed the humanity of Jesus.

In the 1972 *Study of Generations,* which reported on the beliefs of members of U.S. Lutheran churches, a similar finding occurred.[7] The average church member (or ordinary citizen) tended to affirm Christ's divinity but shied away from acknowledging his human nature. For some reason, by contrast, members of Congress are able to take the more orthodox view of Christ's dual nature.

Both Congress (80 percent) and the public (72 percent) view Scripture as the Word of God. That is, they believe that Scripture records what God wanted to be communicated. Hidden inside this seeming consensus are important differences. Some claim that the Bible is completely without error (inerrant). The question of inerrancy is an important dividing principle among some groups. It becomes for them a key test of faith, or of loyalty to a tradition. Within recent memory seminaries have split apart over the demand that an inerrant view of Scripture be taught. We hear television and radio evangelists demanding an inerrant view of Scripture. Because of the attention given this issue nationally, we wanted to compare the *inerrancy rates* for Congress and the public.

There are two general positions taken on the truth of Scripture. Position A holds that the Bible is a document that communicates principles, ideas, the basic truth about the nature of God, and the record of the way in which God has worked with the human race throughout history. People who hold position

Table 5-1

Religious Belief	Our Data on Congress	Gallup's Data on the American Public
Believe in God*		
Yes	95%	94%
No	4%	4%
Don't know	1%	2%
Beliefs about Jesus**		
Jesus Christ is divine	71%	83%
Jesus Christ is divine		
and human	68%	25%
Scripture as Word of God***		
The Bible is the Word of God	80%	72%
The Bible is a collection of		
fables and stories	7%	23%
Do not know, uncertain	9%	5%
Other	4%	—
Belief in life after death†		
Yes	81%	69%
No	9%	20%
Uncertain	10%	11%

*The percentage for Congress in the *yes* category represents a combination of the two categories *I definitely believe* and *I am uncertain, but lean toward believing*. For the Gallup data, see *Christianity Today*, December 21, 1979, pp. 14–15.

**Three percent of Congress believe *Jesus is divine but not human*. When added to the 68 percent who believe *Jesus is divine and human*, a total of 71 percent can be said to affirm the divinity of Jesus. The Gallup figure of 83 percent is found in Kenneth S. Kantzer, "The Charismatics among Us," *Christianity Today*, February 22, 1980, p. 27. The 25 percent figure was calculated using information provided in *Christianity Today*, December 21, 1979, p. 15.

***The Gallup figure can be found in Princeton Religious Research Center (53 Bank Street, Princeton, NJ 08540), *Emerging Trends*, May 1980, p. 3. The 72 percent figure is slightly higher than the 69 percent that was reported in the December, 1981, issue of *Psychology Today*. The lower figure came from an earlier Gallup publication.

†The Gallup figures can be found in the Gallup Opinion Index (Report No. 130), *Religion in America, 1976*, p. 19. Though this seems to be "older" data, Gallup notes on p. 18 of this report that the percentage of Americans who believe in life after death has remained remarkably stable since 1948.

A say that it is not important whether all the characters mentioned in the Scriptures actually said and did all the things attributed to them exactly as recorded. Proponents of position A usually grant that some of the concrete detail may well have become altered in the reporting.

Position B holds that everything in Scripture is true and factual as stated, including all specific details. It indeed rained for forty days and forty nights at the time of the Great Flood; it took six twenty-four-hour days to create the world; the words recorded as being spoken by the serpent to Eve were actually uttered; and Jonah spent three days and nights inhabiting the digestive tract of a great fish. These are believed to be truths in the sense of their being historical facts; things happened exactly the way Scripture records it.

Where are the members of Congress on this issue? In the congressional interview we first asked whether everything in Scripture is absolutely true and factual. If the response did not sufficiently clarify the member's position, we asked further questions. We found that 15 percent of the members take position B, with a strong majority of 69 percent taking position A. Overall, then, 84 percent believe that Scripture is true, but only a small minority go so far as to affirm the totally inerrant view of position B.

How widespread in the public is belief in inerrancy? It is difficult to obtain a strictly comparable figure for the general public. Gallup says that in the general public we can find 42 percent[8] agreeing with the inerrant view (position B). That is the percentage who said yes to this statement: The Bible is the Word of God and never mistaken. It seems to us that this question does not clearly separate persons who hold position B from some who hold position A. There are at least some in position A who believe that the general truth conveyed in the Bible is accurate and who might well respond in the affirmative to the Gallup question, wanting to assent to the first half of the question, and interpreting in a general way the meaning of *and never mistaken.*

It obviously makes a difference how a question is phrased. The Roper Organization, commissioned by the National Broadcasting Company in 1981 to study public attitudes toward television programming, phrased the question differently. They asked of a random sample of Americans, "Is Scripture the

Word of God and recorded with no mistakes?"9 Only 27 percent agreed to this phrasing, a figure more comparable with, though almost twice as large as, our 15 percent figure for the champions of inerrancy in Congress.

Does Congress practice religion to the same extent as the general public? If the seven issues listed in table 5-2 adequately measure religious behavior, we can answer yes to this question. On the average members pray, read Scripture, and attend church as often as the public. Note, however, that although the averages for Congress and the public are similar, the distribution is different. For each of these three behaviors fewer members appear at the extreme highs or extreme lows. More of the public say they attend church more than once a week, pray twice a day or more, or read Scripture daily. But, at the same time, the public is more heavily represented in the never-pray, never-read-Scripture, and rarely-attend-church categories. The public has more representatives at the high and low extremes of religious practice.

A higher proportion of members of Congress are at least moderately practicing, as compared with the public. Seventy-four percent of members attend church at least once a month, compared with 50 percent of the public; 53 percent read Scripture once a month or more, compared with 48 percent of the public; and 95 percent pray sometimes, compared with 89 percent of the public. On the importance-of-religion item, 93 percent of members attest to religion being at least fairly important, compared with 84 percent of the public. The differences are not large, but in all four cases Congress appears to have a higher proportion that pays some attention to religion.

A particularly noticeable contrast occurs with respect to church membership. More members of Congress (90 percent) belong to a church or synagogue than do members of the public (67 percent). There may not be a meaningful difference here. Being a member of a church is politically expedient: people expect it and raise their eyebrows if they find that a candidate is not a church member. So whether church membership measures religious or political motivations is not clear.

Just as Congress is not at either extreme in religious involvement, it is not extreme in its theological loyalties. Congress does

Table 5-2

Religious Behavior and Experience	Our Data on Congress	Gallup's Data on the American Public
Member of a church or synagogue*		
Yes	90%	67%
No	10%	33%
Church Attendance**		
More than once a week	3%	11%
Weekly	29%	25%
One to three times a month	42%	14%
Less than once a month	26%	50%
Scripture reading***		
Daily	5%	11%
Once a week or more, but less than daily	32%	19%
One to three times a month	16%	18%
Less than once a month	33%	28%
Never	13%	24%
Do you pray?†		
Yes	95%	89%
No	5%	11%
Have had a born-again experience‡	30%	34%
Have spoken in tongues (glossolalia)#	3%	4%
Importance of religion in my life##		
Very important	52%	57%
Fairly important	41%	27%
Not too important	3%	11%
Not at all important	4%	4%

*Gallup figures are from *Christianity Today*, December 21, 1979, p. 16.

**Gallup figures were calculated from data presented in *Christianity Today*, December 21, 1979, pp. 14 and 16.

***Gallup figures were calculated from data presented in *Christianity Today*, December 21, 1979, p. 14, February 22, 1980, p. 27.

†*Emerging Trends*, January, 1981, p. 3.

‡Gallup figures from Princeton Religion Research Center, *Religion in America, 1977–1978*, p. 43.

#Gallup figures from *Religion in America, 1979–1980*, p. 36.

##Congressional figures represent classifications based on the religious lifeline question discussed in the previous chapter. Those members whose lifeline ended at 10 or above were classified as *very important*; 7–9, *fairly important*; 3–6, *not too important*; 0–2, *not at all important*. The Gallup figures are from *Religion in America, 1979–1980*, p. 23.

not have many members who can be called Pentecostal or char-
ismatic. Few volunteered comments about the Holy Spirit and
the "gifts of the Spirit," as persons identified with these two
movements tend to do. We did not attempt to secure information about these two orientations, but we would estimate that
the Pentecostal/charismatic orientation is considerably less characteristic of members of Congress than the 19 percent figure
Gallup claims for the public.[10]

Another religious orientation much talked about in recent
years in America is Eastern. There has been much media attention to practitioners of Buddhist and Hindu religious forms.
Gallup reports, though, that only 1 percent of Americans are
involved in these movements.[11] In our congressional sample we
found no members actively engaged in an Eastern religious
form, though several had appropriated the concept of reincarnation and integrated it into an otherwise Christian perspective.
And, in addition, a surprisingly large number (25 percent)
chose a description of the relationship of God to the world ("the
world is part of God, but God is greater and larger than the
world") that fits more naturally into Eastern concepts than into
Western ones.

At nearly all the points at which we have been able to compare them, Congress not only is as religious as the American
public, but in some areas shows greater religious interest, practicing some of the standard religious-behavior activities with
greater frequency than the general public.

The Myth in Focus

> *Myth Number Two:* Members of Congress are
> less religious than the people they serve.

The evidence is clear that Congress well reflects the dominant religious beliefs and behaviors present among the American public. It is not true, as some contend, that the members of
Congress are less religious than the people they serve. The
more warranted conclusion is that Congress is at least as religious as the public. And this conclusion is based on comparing

a Congress that is 90 percent male and about 90 percent college educated with a public that is only about 50 percent male and college educated. In most research on religion it is found that men generally show less religious interest than women and that religious commitment decreases as education increases. Were we to compare Congress with college-educated men only, we would probably find that members of Congress are more religious than their counterparts in the public.

The myth that Congress is not very religious exists primarily outside of Congress, not inside. Since December, 1981, when some of our findings were published in *Psychology Today*,[12] we have had opportunity to discuss with a number of people the comparison of Congress and the public. Two reactions are common: people in Congress, their staff, and some media people who cover Congress say, "What's new about that? I knew many in Congress were strongly religious." People outside Washington say, "I find it hard to believe that Congress can be so strongly religious. Don't you think they were lying to you?" At the beginning of this chapter we noted that no poll on public perception of religion among members of Congress has been taken. If any meaning can be attached to the informal comments made thus far about our findings, it would be that the public believes that Congress is low on the religious dimension.

Those who assume that members of Congress are low on religious interest and activity have generated a stereotype based on faulty inferences. The public knows about Congress chiefly through what it hears or reads. And it hears or reads mostly about the swindlers and cheaters and liars, because bad news is news and good news is not. Stories about illicit sex and money in brown paper bags make better copy than stories about members who have taught Sunday School for twenty years or are serving on a committee to choose a new rabbi for the congregation. Because the media focus more on vice than on virtue,[13] the average citizen comes to believe that the stories he or she hears about Congress are commonplace happenings.

How does this connect to the belief that Congress is not very religious? It is part of the American consciousness to assume that religion and morality go hand in hand: where there is religion there is morality, and where there is no religion there is no morality. The evidence on this matter is equivocal. But what matters is that people think it is true.

Armed with an overestimate of immoral behavior among members and the assumption that morality comes from religious commitment, the public underestimates the religious commitments of members. As one person put it after hearing some of our findings, "Your results must be wrong. There's no way, with all the rotten things congressmen do, that they can be *that* religious."

To that we propose this alternative. A great many members of Congress are involved with religious belief and activity. Though a few are conspicuously low in virtue, it is incorrect to assume that what is true of the publicized few is true of all. If, as the public believes, religion and morality go hand in hand, then the new information we present—that Congress is by and large religious—compels us to reevaluate our national stereotype about the morality (or lack of it) among our legislators.

6. Is the Vision of America's Founders Still Alive?

Lo! the angel Gabriel comes.
From him that sits upon the throne;
All nations hear the great Jehovah's will;
America, henceforth separate,
Sit as Queen among the nations.

—JOHN DEVOTION[1]

M O S T   O F us think of the American Revolution as a military struggle with England, beginning with our declaration of autonomy and culminating in surrender by the British troops. But more than a political revolution was in process. Running parallel to these historic nation-forming events was an equally dramatic revolution in religious ideas. This religious revolution may, in fact, have played an important role in leading the early patriots to victory.

The religious revolution swept through the colonies in the latter half of the eighteenth century. It provided a world view that transcended the theological and cultural schisms commonplace from New England to the Carolinas. It provided a justification for claiming and fighting for independence and created a sense of shared mission and purpose. Without this national ideology the colonists might well have been too divided to work together successfully for independence. In this chapter, we will describe this nation-building religion and then examine whether our current national leaders have kept this patriotic faith alive. Does the vision that united us then give us direction now?

It must be acknowledged at the outset that in dealing with the beliefs of America's founders we have only the surviving writings and public statements of these men, along with the subsequent judgments of historians, to inform us. (It is said that history tends to be written by men about men, so that much of this country's early history has a predominantly male imprint. The full history of the significant contributions of women has yet to be written.) We lack the opportunity to inquire into, probe, and analyze the shape of the personal religious beliefs of these figures of history that we have with present-day legislators. All we have to work from is their (presumably) carefully prepared public statements. Some students of religious history suggest that these public statements were shaped more by political expedience than by personal conviction. We cannot judge the truth of that hypothesis. We only acknowledge the risk of error involved in comparing the belief system outlined in the founders' public statements with the personal statements given by present-day members of Congress.

In drawing this portrait of religion among America's founders, we look for the prominent themes that characterize their writings. Not all of the early leaders shared each of the beliefs described in this chapter. There was among them, indeed, some diversity of belief. Accordingly, the beliefs we describe here are the themes that emerge as dominant, but not always held by all.

The Historical Setting

The religious ideas that came to prominence two hundred years ago quite naturally influenced the political ideas of America's founders. The new religious ideas captured the minds and hearts of both the educated classes—essayists, poets, clergy, politicans—and the common people. Certainly, men like George Washington, Benjamin Franklin, and Thomas Jefferson spoke for the new religion and helped to disseminate it among the masses. They did not invent it. They gravitated to it, adopting it either from conviction or for its utilitarian value. With it they built a national consciousness and made it the ideological cornerstone of the Declaration of Independence and the Constitution. The theological principles of this nation-building religion are thus part of our national heritage.

To understand the new, nation-building religion, it is crucial first to understand the three strains from which it developed— the Puritanism of white America's earliest history, the Great Awakening of the early eighteenth century, and the Age of Enlightenment of the mid-eighteenth century. Perhaps no heritage was more pervasive in impact or support than Puritanism. "Approximately three-fourths of the colonists at the time of the Revolution were identified with denominations that had arisen from the Reformed, Puritan wing of European Protestantism: Congregationalism, Presbyterian, Baptists, German and Dutch Reformed."[2] Puritanism was a stringent, Bible-believing religious heritage which vigorously translated theological perspectives into a detailed, rigorous moral code, which was related both to individuals and to corporate life. Puritans felt called it take active part in the social and political world, shaping it to conform to the dictates of God's divine plan. Puritans were staunch defenders of individual liberty and believed it proper to protect that liberty through political means. The new nation-building religion that evolved later grew out of these liberty-seeking, politically active roots, finding them a firm foundation for the spiritual revolution to come.

This Puritan heritage was a religion that looks now to us rather colorless and mechanical. It was, by and large, ecclesiastical, formal, stringent, divisive, and as Jonathan Edwards said, "extraordinarily dull."[3] In the early 1700s a religious movement began which touched every nook and cranny of the colonies. It was called the Great Awakening, and its impact was strong and far reaching. It was a movement that stressed personal experience, the heart rather than the head. The experience of feeling God's presence, feeling redeemed, was highly valued. The movement had some similarities to our current evangelical movement.

By 1740 the Great Awakening had "spread throughout every colony from Nova Scotia to Georgia to touch every area—urban and rural, tidewater and backcountry—and every class—rich and poor, educated and uneducated—before its power was finally dissipated."[4] The immediate effect of this movement was divisive. It split congregations and denominations. But in the long run it played a major role in building a national unity. As Hudson described it:

The Awakening was much more than the activity of a few conspicuous leaders. It was "Great" because it was general.... And because the

Awakening was general, it played an important role in forming a national consciousness among people of different colonies whose primary ties were with Europe rather than with one another. As a spontaneous movement which swept across all colonial boundaries, generated a common interest and a common loyalty, bound people together in a common cause, and reinforced the conviction that God had a special destiny in store for America, the Awakening contributed greatly to the development of a sense of cohesiveness among the American people.[5]

The strains of Puritanism and the Great Awakening were joined in the mid-eighteenth century by another set of ideas representing what is called the Age of Enlightenment. It introduced to the nation a revised picture of human nature and human capability. Indeed, it might be called the original human-potential movement. It was an intellectual mood that swept through the entire Western world during the eighteenth century. New advances in science triggered new respect for the capability of the human mind. European societies had by and large been premised on the notion that the enlightened few must govern the uneducated, ignorant masses. It was thought appropriate for social control to work from the top down, and for everyone to occupy a well-defined place in society. The new Enlightenment's optimism about human nature challenged the notion that the average citizen could not lead a responsible life without authorities constantly looking over his shoulder.

This optimistic mood set the stage for radical thinking in politics and religion. "Human suffering and submission to tyranny —whatever the source—were no longer to be accepted supinely as the natural form of political existence. The divine right of kings was to be re-examined and resisted."[6] These new ideas became central to the American intellectual elite, including those public figures who became known as the founders. Individual liberty became the ultimate virtue; coercion and oppression were viewed as ultimate evil.

The impact of Enlightenment ideas on political thinking was no more dramatic than it was on religious thinking. Cousins describes the common theme in the intellectual evolution of the founders:

Theology became an especially inviting arena for lay inquiry and exploration. For the more men probed the universe, and the more they became acquainted with the wonder of life itself, the more interested they became in a first cause. . . . When they questioned denominational religion, it was not because they questioned the spiritual urge in man but because they felt, many of them, that the evolutionary development of religion had not kept pace with the expanding horizons of human intellect and progress. And though most of them resisted the literal Biblical view of creation, they maintained respect for the Bible as the source of Judaeo-Christian religious belief. They were opposed to legislation that sought literal acceptance of Biblical interpretation of the universe and man's place in it. Similarly, they were opposed to laws—which actually existed in several of the American states—making church attendance compulsory. Man's approach to God, they believed, was as personal as his own soul.[7]

These three broad cultural movements had combined to leave their mark on America, and hence on the framers of the national destiny. The Puritan heritage justified the pursuit of liberty and the involvement of religious people in the political arena. The Great Awakening sowed the seeds of national unity, providing for the young colonists a foundation on which to build a national religio-political consensus. And the Enlightenment offered a new view of human possibilities and created a readiness for—if not an insistence on—massive political change.

By the mid-eighteenth century, America was ready for a new religio-political synthesis. The new religion, built on the foundation of Puritanism, the Great Awakening, and the Enlightenment, wove the varied strands together and created a world view that spread from the educated elite to the masses. It gave America a place in the divine scheme and provided supernatural justification for the break with England and the eventual military conflict.

The Nation-Building Religion

This new nation-building religion has been given many names. It has been called *national religion*,[8] *republican religion*,[9] *civil religion*,[10] and *enlightened Christianity*.[11] Whatever its name, the belief system has three components: God, the divine plan, and the social contract.

God

As optimism grew about the potential of human intelligence, something had to be done about the existing concept of God. God had been the central figure in the scheme of things; and persons, seen as wallowing in depravity, depended mightily on God for all things. But as people were liberated from the conviction of depravity and became more central figures in the universe, their concept of God's nature and involvement changed. They began to put less emphasis on God's active role in human events. No longer the constant provider and immanent presence, God became the Great Architect, the Author, the Creator. People became primary, "while God was more and more relegated to the conventionalities, a kind of cosmic backdrop which did not interfere in the everyday conduct of human affairs."[12]

The shift to deism (a concept defined in chapter 3) became increasingly popular. God created the universe, set the world on its course, and sat back to watch it unfold. It was a shift in thought, not an absolute change. That is, the common concept of God became more deistic in flavor, but not totally so. In fact, the patriots mixed their God-images in convenient but inconsistent ways. When justification was needed for the assertion that the patriots had the right to challenge existing civil and ecclesiastical authority, it was helpful to see God as one who was removed enough to allow the early Americans to shape their own lives and fortunes. But when things were going badly, it became convenient to resurrect the God of history who intervened in the course of events and lent a hand in military combat.[13]

The Divine Plan

The Great Architect was not, by virtue of his assumed inactivity, considered unimportant. It became of paramount importance to discover the divine plan and, through the exercise of reason and free will, to attempt to follow it. Since God had designed nature so skillfully, the plan was obvious to anyone who cared to look. One did not have to turn to Scripture, miracles, the church, or the life of Jesus, as in ages past, to see God's will. Now, reason and scientific knowledge could provide necessary insights into the religious, ethical, and political forms that God intended to govern human life. No one captured this sentiment better than Thomas Jefferson:

I hold (without appeal to revelation) that when we take a view of the universe, in its parts, general or particular, it is impossible for the human mind not to perceive and feel a conviction of design, consummate skill, and infinite power in every atom of its composition. . . . We see, too, evident proofs of the necessity of a superintending power, to maintain the universe in its couse and order.[14]

What was this divine plan which could be understood through reason? It had three components:

1. *Recognition of a higher law.* God, not government, is the final authority. Civil power stands under the sovereignty of God and "the nation must judge its own acts in the light of divine righteousness."[15] The nation, or any nation, is then not an end in itself "but stands under transcendent judgment and has value only insofar as it realizes, partially and fragmentarily at best, a 'higher law.' "[16]

2. *Minimal governmental interference.* This higher law includes the notion of human liberty or freedom. As God is free to act, so are people. Accordingly, any governmental form which coerced persons into subjugation to human authorities was judged to be outside God's will. Reason dictated that God had given people inalienable human rights. Freedom was seen as part of natural human endowment. Persons could consent to government as a way to preserve and protect liberty. But an authoritarian government that forced obedience was evil. The message was clear: British rule of the colonies as it was carried out (e.g., taxation without representation) was outside God's plan.

These theological premises have no better proclamation than in the opening lines of the Declaration of Independence:

We hold these truths to be self-evident, that all Men are created equal, that they are endowed by their Creator with certain unalienable Rights, that among these are Life, Liberty, and the Pursuit of Happiness—That to secure these Rights, Governments are instituted among Men deriving their just Powers from the Consent of the Governed . . .[17]

3. *America as symbol of freedom.* This was more than a general invitation to the people of the world to fight the battle of liberty against menacing governmental forms. The divine plan for human liberty preserved by a government of consent was specially designed for America.

Even prior to the war some Americans were audacious enough to believe that the colonists alone were God's new Israel. After the war this became the general conviction. Through his providential control of events, God had fashioned the United States as a new instrument to effect his purposes for mankind. Thomas Jefferson, Benjamin Franklin, John Adams, and other members of the Constitutional Convention were as vigorous as any clergyman in asserting that the United States had come into being as a grand design of Providence for "the illumination of the ignorant and the emancipation of the slavish part of mankind over all the earth."[18]

America was the Promised Land, the new Israel, called by God to be a light to the world, proclaiming the right of all people to liberty and freedom. The promised kingdom of glory would be erected in America. The new America would shine, a beacon for all to see, and with it, reshape the world.

To the perfection of this work, a great example is required of which the world may take knowledge, and which shall inspire hope and rouse and concentrate the energies of man. But where could such a nation be found? It must be created for it had no existence upon the earth. Look now at the history of our fathers and behold what God hath wrought . . . , a powerful nation in full enjoyment of civil and religious liberty, where all the energies of men . . . find scope and excitement on purpose to show the world by experiment of what man is capable. . . . When the light of such a hemisphere shall go up to the heavens it will throw its beams beyond the waves; . . . it will awaken desire and hope and effort and produce revolutions and overturnings until the world is free.[19]

The Social Contract

The deal God struck with America, as the founders expressed it, was two-sided. On one side was God's pledge of support if America lived up to the sacred trust. God would heap blessings on America if it followed the script. America could expect victory in battle, protection of the new government and its institutions, individual happiness, and material bounty. America was the Promised Land flowing with milk and honey, and Europe was Egypt. God entrusted to America a special role in the world—and if we lived up to that role, God was on our side.

That America would follow the divine plan was not automatically programmed into the world's atoms and molecules. God expected conformity to the plan but built free will into the system so that, theoretically, America could go a different course. If America failed in its mission, divine displeasure could quickly bring divine judgment upon the nation.[20]

George Washington clearly spoke of both sides of this contract: the potential blessings and the potential wrath. In his first inaugural address on April 30, 1789, he said:

The propitious smiles of Heaven can never be expected on a nation that disregards the eternal rules of order and right which Heaven itself has ordained. . . . The preservation of the sacred fire of liberty and the destiny of the republican model of government are justly considered, perhaps as deeply, as finally, staked on the experiment intrusted to the hands of the American people.[21]

These three new understandings—of God, the divine plan, and the social contract—were woven together to create a religio-political world view that spread quickly through the colonies. Certainly not all persons completely subscribed to all these premises. Many, including some of the founders, held on to a more orthodox Christian faith which ran parallel to, or was integrated with, the new nation-building faith. But the essential elements—that God had called America to be a light to the world (for liberty, freedom, and limited government) and blessed it with great prosperity—became commonplace images among both the elite and the common people.

It was a world view that bound the nation together, cutting through the theological and cultural divisions of the day. It provided an overarching supernatural myth for creating a new nation. For a variety of reasons, the nation became immensely optimistic, believing that under God's providential hand the path led steadily upward.

The Nation-Building Religion in Present-Day Congress

Is God the Great Architect?

In chapter 3, we explored members' beliefs about God. One conclusion was that members emphasize God's immanence (closeness) as much as his transcendence. The vast majority attribute to God ultimate power and goodness. But God is not just "out there" watching history pass by. Rather, God's transcendence, emphasized in the nation-building religion, is balanced with an equally emphasized account of his consistent activity in history and human lives. Most of our legislators use personal, relational terms to describe how God works in human lives. They are not describing the impersonal God of deism. The image is of an attentive God, to some a Companion God. This is one way in which the God-image of contemporary legislators differs from that found in the writings of the founders.

There are two other notable differences. When it comes to the question of how God is known, only a minority attest to finding God predominantly by looking at the design and order of creation. Most see God through revelation, not reason.

Nor do current legislators sound like the founders when they describe the arena of God's activity. Two hundred years ago, particularly at the start of the Revolution, the emphasis was on God's relationship to the nation. God called the nation, blessed the nation, saved the nation. Certainly, some patriots also recognized God's activity in individual lives. But the relationship to the corporate body was almost always present, not unlike the kind of relationship depicted between God and Israel in Old Testament literature. In today's Congress few see God actively at work with the nation as a whole. Today the view in Congress, as with the public, is that God calls, blesses, and saves the individual. God is not the nation-saver: God is the person-saver. Faith is not a corporate, national experience; it is a private, individual experience. This is a radical change. It began early in the nineteenth century when a new evangelical movement swept across the nation as an attack on the intellectual God of Nature. What probably happened is that once the

American Revolution was won, the identity of the individual began to shift from being part of a corporate we're-in-this-together theme, in which individual needs were subservient to the common good, to a more self-centered theme consistent with the new nation's emphasis on the sanctity of individual liberty and self-expression. There is no doubt that identity in American society continues now to be premised more on "me" than on "we." Accordingly, God is experienced more in personal terms than in corporate terms.

Is America Central in God's Divine Plan?

Had social scientists polled the nation two hundred years ago, the vast majority would likely have said yes to the statement that God has chosen America to be a light to the world. A dark cloud hung over most of the world at that time. Light was an apt symbol for freedom and liberty—conditions of life not common anywhere in the known world. Only 24 percent now strongly agree with this statement. (See table 6-1.) To some of the detractors it is an arrogant, ethnocentric statement which deserves to die. To some whose relationship with God is a very personally experienced one, the idea that God works at the national level to choose, direct, or motivate nations simply does not make sense.

Table 6-1

Statement	Percentage Who Gave This Response
God has chosen America to be a light to the world. How true is this statement?	
True	24
Not sure, but lean toward true	11
Not sure, but lean toward false	7
Not true	49
Don't know or can't answer	9

To those affirming the statement we asked, "A light for what?" All said that America was chosen as an example of either individual liberty or a nation founded on God (a reminder of the higher-law principle). There was one surprise. None mentioned America as a liberator of the oppressed or a haven for the weak and tired. Two hundred years ago these were among the most common understandings of the role which God had chosen for America.

To many of the founders salvation took on a here-and-now flavor. There was a widespread belief that the millennium was at hand and that God had chosen America as the seat of God's earthly rule. Among current legislators this new-kingdom aspect of salvation has been lost in favor of salvation conceived as individual immortality. This switch provides another illustration of how religion has changed from a corporate emphasis to an individual one.

Is the Contract between God and America Still Viable?

The contract between the nation and God, as understood in the late eighteenth century, had two sides. Compliance with the divine plan merited national prosperity; noncompliance led to judgment. The patriots were certain of their compliance, and equally certain that God responded by lavishing both natural and political blessings on America. God's expectations for America were being met, and the new nation prospered. A solid minority of contemporary members affirm the statement: God has blessed America more than other nations. (See table 6-2.) A nearly equal number reject it. Overall, there is no longer any widespread consensus on this issue.

No one in Congress appears to believe that God has let us

Table 6-2

Statement	Percentage Who Chose This Response
God has blessed America more than other nations. How true is this statement?	
True	32
Not sure, but lean toward true	10
Not sure, but lean toward false	5
False	38
Don't know or can't answer	14

down. Instead, we found a rather frequently voiced comment that America has not lived up to its end of the contract. We asked each member to say how well he or she thought America is now meeting God's expectations for what a society should be. (See table 6-3.)

Table 6-3

Statement	Percentage Who Chose This Response
A. America is very close to fulfilling God's expectations	7
B. America is very far from fulfilling God's expectations	57
C. Somewhere between *A* and *B*	15
D. Far away, but closer than other nations	10
E. Can't choose—God does not have expectations for America	6
F. Don't know	5

The majority selected option *B*. Only 7 percent directly affirmed position *A*. We do not know if the members of Congress really believe that God established a covenant with America which is now in jeopardy. But we can safely infer that those who chose *B* are saying that they do not see all proceeding well in a land flowing with milk and honey. This represents a dramatic change in mood; speeches and writings of the patriots were filled with optimism, espousing the view that God's expectations were being met. Current lawmakers view American society with more pessimism—some might say more realism—believing there is a wide gap between what we are and what we might be.

For How Many Members Is the Vision Alive?

How many of today's lawmakers subscribe to the founders' religious vision? The answer to this question depends on how strict we are in defining the essential ingredients of the original nation-building theology. Few members today adopt the kind of deistic view of God popular in the late eighteenth century. Deism was at that time a frequent component of beliefs about the divine plan and the contract. But it was not an essential ingredient. It seems to us that the most central tenets of the nation-building religion were the two we asked members about: God has chosen America to be a light to the world, and God has blessed America more than other nations. Less than 30 percent of current members affirm both of these statements simultaneously. It would seem that the founders' religious ideology is now a minority view.

We noted earlier that the divine plan included several messages about the shape of government. The new nation was to stand under "higher law." In part, this meant that the nation and its laws should conform to God's laws. Secondly, the new nation was to be set up so that individual liberty was maximized and government interference in everyday life (what the founders called *coercion*) was minimized. To know whether a person is truly adhering to the founders' religious vision, we must know if those political sentiments are also adhered to. We did not ask members directly about the higher-law and minimal-interference aspects of the divine plan. But we can infer adherence by examining members' voting behavior. The New Christian Right declares that abortion and homosexuality are violations of God's higher law. This political movement justifies government coercion in these moral matters by appealing to claims about God's will. Further, the New Christian Right sees expansion of the federal government into social programs based on the principle of taxing the "haves" to aid the "have-nots" as unnecessary (and ungodly) violations of individual liberty. We examined the degree to which beliefs that "God has blessed America more than other nations" and "God has chosen America to be a light to the world" correlated with voting on abortion, homosexuality, and government spending. We found that the correlations are strong: the greater the adherence to the two beliefs about God's intent for America, the greater the likelihood that a member votes against abortion, against civil liberties for homosexuals, and against government spending for social programs.[22] Overall, about 20 percent of the members in our sample adhere to the dual blessed-America-more and light-to-the-world beliefs and, at the same time, vote in ways that reflect a commitment to the principles of higher law and minimal government interference. Thus, the nation-building religion prominent two hundred years ago has only minor influence now.

At the time of the founders, the new religious vision fueled the revolution and helped bring about massive social change. In contemporary terms, adherence to the light-to-the-world and God-has-blessed-America beliefs is associated with conservative politics. Not only are the correlations strong with traditionally conservative mandates for minimal governmental and moral restrictions, but they are also strongly related to voting for increased military expenditures and against foreign aid.[23]

As these latter two relationships to voting suggest, belief in the original divine plan is associated with nationalism. It was two hundred years ago, and it still is. Few in 1776 stood out against a nationalism that built and strengthened the new America by claiming and fighting for independence. Nationalism today, defined as creating a strong military fortress against the threats of the outside world, is another matter—still nationalism, but with different implications. There is no doubt that in contemporary times there is more division in Congress over whether this kind of nationalism is entirely good.

The vision of America that emerges from the writing and speeches of America's founders is a minority view now. Should we mourn its decline? It depends on where one stands. Those who long for a return to traditional values may well feel a sense of loss. Those who desire an America that takes care of its social victims—and are willing to intervene in social life to make this happen—may well celebrate its malaise.

Some say that a nation needs an overarching, supernaturally connected vision to unite its people and give it purpose and direction. If the original nation-building myth no longer works, does America need to create a new one? What would this new myth look like? An androgynous God who gives us new perspective on things male and female? A God of unity who calls the nation to racial equality? One contemporary thinker has proposed that nation-maintaining myths are now counterproductive. In this view what is needed is a global myth, capable of uniting the world's people around a common mission.[24]

Members of Congress currently are more united in their distress about the nation's condition than they are in interpreting either the will of God or the will of the people. If the solution does not lie in resurrecting the original nation-building faith, where does it lie? In the next chapter, we explore what members consider to be the most important changes America needs.

7. Dreams for America

Ah, but a man's reach should exceed his grasp,
Or what's a heaven for?
—ROBERT BROWNING, *"Andrea del Sarto"*

INTERVIEWS often do better at eliciting what is most deeply engrained in the thoughts of the interviewee when they offer a broadly focused question, rather than one with a tightly limited focus. Tightly limited questions such as "On a scale of one to five, how important. . . ?" or "Is this statement true or false?" provide excellent material for statistical analysis; such answers slide into the computer like oiled silk. Broad-focus questions gather data that enter the computer awkwardly, if at all, but that may be more revealing to the heart than to the analytical mind. One such question was this: If you had the power to change one thing in America, what would it be?

With this power-to-change-America question, which occurred very late in the interview, the interviewee was offered an opportunity to articulate some of the poetry of the soul. The interviewee was invited to state the dreams that exceed the grasp, but that might define that person's "heaven" in a less restricted context than the heaven-or-hell question asked elsewhere in the interview.

The question was in no sense considered peripheral. In the rigorous revision that occurred when the realities of congressional life were made clear and the interview was pared from a leisurely forty-five minutes to a spartan fifteen or twenty minutes, everything peripheral was jettisoned. But because of this question's broad focus, it was not expected to gather responses that would cluster with many other responses to produce a scale. Neither was it specifically designed to probe any of the areas of hypothesis that the project was designed to explore. Instead, it was considered important of itself; it was considered a question likely to bring to the surface the deepest interests and hopes of the interviewee.

If you had the power to change one thing in America, what would it be? For most this was a difficult question. They paused, stumbled, said, "I suppose I probably should give more thought to this, but ..." or "Oh, Lord. There are so many things ..." A few never were able to formulate an answer. Some asked permission to return to the question later, but the return never occurred, and one simply said, "I don't think I can answer that one."

Another way in which difficulty was made apparent was in the interviewee's repeating the question, putting emphasis on the number ("Change *one* thing?"), as if pleading for permission to name a list rather than make a single choice.

Certainly the question was not the kind they meet every day. Often under pressure of time to make decisions quickly on a variety of practical issues, they become used to thinking in terms of immediate decisions rather than in terms of ultimate goals. In spite of their difficulty with it, members gave the impression that it was a question they rather enjoyed turning over in their minds.

Most members answered the question. The answers ranged from a single word to lengthy paragraphs, from matters of personal morality to world issues, from unattainable goals to practical issues that might move toward solution within the member's lifetime. And yet, in the midst of that variety there were also a good many dreams held in common.

Unselfishness

Of the people interviewed, 35 percent said their dream was that people would become less selfish, less preoccupied with their own well-being and their own little worlds, in order to take a larger, more generous view of life. Several hoped that there would develop among the citizenry an increased sense of responsibility for the country as a whole. Others dreamed that people might become more loving, more tolerant of others' differences and opinions; and a few spoke of their hopes for a reduction in the spirit of competition, with an accompanying increase in the spirit of cooperation and unselfishness.

I think people are very self-centered. I know I can talk [to visitors from my district] about the problem, the big picture, how we all have to contribute. Everyone says, "You're right—but while I'm here, take care of my problem." "I don't want to wait in the gas line." "I don't want to sacrifice. . . ."

Another exchange carries the flavor of the human interaction that was part of the interview context:

Interviewer: If you could change one thing about America, if you had the power to do that, what might your dream be? [Long pause.] It's not the kind of thing it's easy to start Monday morning with, is it?

Member: [Laughs.] I . . . I know what I want to say; I'm just trying to verbalize it. I think that I would want people to look at the wealth and the good life they have and be a little bit more willing to share, because I think the bulk of us are extremely well off. . . . And I can't say why, but it seems we're getting more and more . . . antagonistic toward the "have nots." . . . And I wish we could develop a little better understanding that with all we have, just a little sharing would make it so much better.

The power-to-change-America question immediately followed one that invited the interviewee to state whether the best way to approach social problems is by changing the hearts of individuals or by transforming institutions and structures. The placement of that question is likely to have influenced the responses to this question toward a high percentage of those whose one goal would involve the changing of individuals' hearts and attitudes to produce a corporate effect.

[Reflectively.] One thing to change? It would certainly not be governmental or economic. If there were some way to generate a pervasive sense of sacrifice, a real willingness to care, I think it would right an awful lot of the societal problems we've got.

Change in the Social Environment

The second most frequently mentioned wish, one voiced by 30 percent of the members, was for some change in society. The two changes mentioned most often in this category were the problem of poverty overcome, and equal opportunity for success available to everyone. Other specifics were the reduc-

tion of crime, of racism, or of the housing problem, and a return of the sense of community.

One set of responses articulated by a number of members in
different ways spoke of a desire for goals that would encourage
growth and learning, the development of the inborn potential
of every American. Not surprisingly, some of them focused on
opportunities for youth.

One thing that I would try to change in society would be the modeling
of young people—the emphasis upon opportunity and the emphasis
upon giving them the tools to guide their own destiny.... The one
thing I believe, if I could, would be to give every kid, after he passes
his sixteenth birthday, the realization that he's got a life to live, . . the
opportunity to be a contributing party of society . . . and make the tools
available to him.

Another response, similar in that it speaks to the needs of a
particular age group, focuses on the other end of the life span
—the elderly.

There is so much human misery associated with people in the twilight
years by virtue of illnesses and prolonged hospitalization; I looked
upon Medicare as a catalytic force to evolve from that. Unfortunately,
we're still struggling, still trying to come up with a formula or system
that would put that human tragedy to rest.

Return to Traditional American Values

Almost 19 percent of the interviewees said that their dreams
take the form of a return to some of the traditional American
values—now, they say, sadly out of fashion. The most frequently mentioned wish was for the return of a widespread willingness to work hard. Next most frequently mentioned was a firm
commitment to home and family. The reestablishment of high
moral values, the restoration of the concept of limited government, and the peace and security of the United States—all these
were also part of the dream.

More love for God and stronger belief in family. Patriotism; more love
for country. Things don't come that easily to this nation. It's got to
have people willing to make sacrifices.

We've got to get back to the old-fashioned virtues of work and thrift and belief in a Supreme Being. Eliminate waste and extravagance and hatred.

Stronger Religious Commitment

Fourteen percent of the members' dreams included theological language. Questions about the nature of God and of the relationship of God to the world had occurred many questions earlier in the interview, yet the theological centering of this group was strong enough to appear in the way they presented their dreams for America:

I think if everybody had Jesus Christ in their . . . being and everybody sincerely followed him, there wouldn't be any problems in the world.

I would just change the hearts of individuals and make them believe in a real way in God.

National and Global Concerns

There were some who focused on the national scene.

Ensure the peace and security of my country.

Greater awareness of what we have [the national material wealth] and the opportunity we have.

I'd deal with the power structure—decentralize it.

And a few spoke of concerns that went beyond the national scene to the global picture.

We would get off our energy-junkie mentality to recognize how fragile the natural resources are on the planet Earth, which includes stopping the consumption of thirty-five acres of land a week for development and all the negative things we do to our environment.

If I had one wish that I could bestow on America, it would be peace for the whole world. That would be number one, above everything else.

I think it would be more awareness of the importance of this country in the world and the role that it has in trying to bring about a better world rather than being too self-centered about our own material well-being.

It is interesting to note—and whether or not it is anything other than interesting we do not know—that slightly fewer than half of the interviewees named a problem, something to be eliminated; slightly more than half named a goal, something positive out there ahead that they hoped would one day be achieved. The problem-oriented responses were often more briefly stated than the goal-oriented ones; it is usually easier to define a problem than to outline a solution.

Here are the words that summarize what a number of members mentioned as chief among the problems facing America: economic injustice, cynicism and the propensity to believe the worst about people, racism, our militaristic bent, our own self-satisfaction, greed, overdependence on government, our insistence on instant satisfaction, and barriers to opportunity for all.

It is worth noting that about half of the problems in the list are matters of attitude, observed by legislators and much on their minds, but not accessible to any known kind of legislation. Here we come on the unspoken acknowledgment that even the powers of the powerful Congress are limited; there are some areas of life they cannot touch.

In hearing the responses to this question, the listener got the impression that many in Congress do indeed cherish dreams for their country. But the dreaming part of their nature would not be immediately apparent. Both interviewers characterized the members they met and interviewed as "realistic, businesslike . . . pretty down-to-earth folks . . . busy, keeping a lot of things going at once." However, said one, "After they've talked awhile, you begin to see the beginnings of real caring and longings that they are able to express. I was impressed with the many for whom the dimension of caring and service is a real motivation."

In their private and reflective moments many in Congress have dreamed their dreams for America, visions perhaps formulated long before they ever got to the halls of power. One heard surprisingly little cynicism among them as they spoke. They are divided on what they see as the primary goals toward which America should strive. But they do indeed cherish dreams. Many of them sounded like people whose dearest wish is that their country be what they believe God intended it to be. Their hope is that even now, even with this blurred and flawed beginning, the reality will sometime match the dream.

8. Six Types of Religion in Congress

W H I L E W E learn a good deal from the units of information that interview questions provide, there is even more to be learned from sets of units that, when taken together, summarize larger characteristics or themes. The congressional interview was constructed to yield thirteen sets of units—scales—by which we are able to measure and describe some important ways in which religion takes shape in people's minds and actions. In this chapter the thirteen scales are described, and then we show, by identifying mixtures of these scales, that there are six very different types of religion in the U.S. Congress. The types have very little to do with one's church affiliation. Rather, the six types—called Legalistic, Self-Concerned, Integrated, People-Concerned, Nontraditional, and Nominal—represent a new way to define how religion operates in one's life.

These scales have statistical reliability—that is, the units that make them up can be shown to have a meaningful relationship to one another. There is greater power in the message given by a scale than by a single unit, since the scale is made up of a number of pieces of information all converging on a central meaning.[1]

The thirteen scales are listed below with brief identification; each scale is described in greater detail on subsequent pages.

Thirteen Religion Scales

The first two scales relate to the *importance* of religion and the institutional church.

Pro-Church—the degree to which one appreciates, participates in, and values the influence of the institutional church

Pro-Religion—the degree of importance the person attaches to religious belief and action

The next three scales deal with *theological emphases.*

Evangelical—concept of a close, loving, accessible God who offers guidance and comfort; Jesus is friend and companion; a born-again experience is characteristic

Christian Orthodoxy—belief in the common tenets of most Christian churches: God as personal being, Christ as divine, and the reality of life after death

Symbolic God—concept of God as vast, unknowable, and largely unapproachable; believer accepts possibility that God may not be unchangeable, but evolving

The final eight scales, we believe, represent something new in their application to religious identity. That is, although they encapsulate issues that have for some time been recognized and discussed, this marks the first development of measures that successfully detect their presence and show how they are evident.[2]

These eight scales describe *religious themes* which seem, at first glance, like opposing pairs. As described they are near-opposites, but as they appear in human lives they are mixed in varying amounts and intensities.

Agentic—the degree to which religion reflects individualism and supports and reinforces the well-being of the individual, the self

Communal—the degree to which religion moves one toward a perception of unity and interdependence with other human beings

Vertical—the degree to which religion is understood as a relationship between the individual person and God

Horizontal—the degree to which religion presses a person to adopt compassionate, caring attitudes and actions

Restricting—the degree to which religion is experienced as supplying limits, control, guidelines, and discipline

Releasing—the degree to which religion is experienced as freeing and enabling

Comfort—the degree to which religion is valued for support, comfort, and solace

Challenge—the degree to which religion is experienced as a spur to action

On the next pages we not only present fuller description of each of the eight, but also tell how each of the themes was manifested in the congressional interview.

Every congressional interviewee was given a score for each of the thirteen scales. The member's score on each is higher or lower as the member gave more or less evidence of the presence of what each scale is measuring.

Eight Religious Themes

Identity: Agentic–Communal

AGENTIC

Create a pure heart in me, O God, and give me a new and steadfast spirit;
do not drive me from thy presence or take thy holy spirit from me;
revive in me the joy of thy deliverance and grant me a willing spirit to uphold me.

Psalm 51:10–12

COMMUNAL

For through faith you are all sons of God in union with Christ Jesus. Baptized into union with him, you have all put on Christ as a garment. There is no such thing as Jew and Greek, slave and freeman, male and female; for you are all one person in Christ Jesus.

Galatians 3:26–29

The first two themes ask the question, How do I think of myself? Do I think of myself as an autonomous, independent person, or do I see myself principally as a part of a network of human relationships?

David Bakan, who gave this pair of themes their names, has devoted a book, *The Duality of Human Existence*,[3] to a discussion of the way in which the Agentic and Communal themes have influenced capitalism, religious expression, male and female roles, and a variety of other matters. He defines Agentic activity as taking firm control over one's own life and decisions as well as seeking influence, direction, and control over the activity of others. It is the Agentic in us that is goal directed, organizing our own lives and the lives of others toward the end of achieving those goals. In the pure Agentic the wants, desires, and purposes of others are not considered or taken into account. The highly Agentic person is individualistic, autonomous, and self-sufficient. Agentics tend toward mastery or dominance over others and constantly seek to expand their sphere of mastery.

An Agentic strides out into the world to make things happen —an independent spirit, individually visible and single-mindedly focused on his or her own success and goals. The stereotype of the highly successful businessman (*man*, since Bakan defines the Agentic style as the usual male role) exercising total control over a far-flung industrial empire and affecting the lives and destinies of thousands is pure Agentic.

In the religious context the Agentic theme reinforces and solidifies a person's tendencies to focus on his/her own needs and plans. There is a lot of "me" in Agentic religion. It is Agentic to think that God is aware of everything one does, observing, monitoring, approving. Agentics believe that God is on their side, protecting them from their enemies and enabling them to be winners. It is Agentic to take seriously one's identity as a child and heir of the King of the Universe, by which one therefore becomes royalty on the earth.

The Communal theme emphasizes a more corporate identity. The self is defined more in a social context, and the goal of life is not so much individuality and separateness, but unity with others, interdependence, a blending of oneself with others. In the religious context the Communal theme sees God working to bring about cooperation and unity. *We* is the word uppermost in the Communal theme. One's religion exists, in part, to help one understand how to bring about a closer bonding among people, how to create a greater sense of community, to which individuality is subservient.

Bakan does not depict Agentic and Communal as equally valued. Much of the trouble of the world, he would say, flows from our human tendency to exaggerate the Agentic in our natures and repress the Communal.

The Agentic Theme in the Congressional Interview

The Agentic theme, in the congressional interview, includes seven units of information, all delivering parts of the same message. When asked about "the human problem," the member defined it as the problem of knowing how to live one's life—a lack of purpose or direction for the individual. The meaning of salvation, or the solution to the human problem, was also described in terms of some individual, personal outcome—often personal guidance or a sense of direction and purpose.

The importance of the individual permeates an Agentic concept of relationships with God. Members who revealed the Agentic theme believe that individual identity is of sufficient importance that it will be preserved after death. They also express the belief that God is aware from moment to moment of everything people think and do and that God acts on these moment-to-moment observations by rewarding or punishing people for what they have done or thought.

Coders and interviewers, rating members' interviews, were asked to place each interviewee on a continuum between self-centered and other-centered.[4] Members placed by coders at the self-centered end turned out to be strongly Agentic on other questions. There is usually a preponderance of self-reference—a good deal of "I"—when a person who scores high on the Agentic scale talks about religion, faith, belief, and God's activity in the world. As the Agentic theme would have it, God's work is done mostly through individual persons, and persons relate individually and directly to God.

The Communal Theme in the Congressional Interview

Members of Congress whose responses play a Communal theme relate their religion strongly to being connected with and responsible for other people. Six units converge to make up this theme. The Communal theme holds that the major human problem, the thing that causes most trouble and pain in life, is human inability to live successfully in interaction and cooperation with others. When we fail it is usually because we have failed in community. The path to salvation comes through exercising caring and compassion for other people, doing good for others. Salvation, or the goal toward which religion directs us, is described in terms that recognize community and connectedness; salvation means establishment of a new order, improvement of the human condition. "Improvement of the human condition" may sound much like "a better, more fulfilled life," which is one of the Agentic definitions of salvation. The difference is that the member who scores high on the Agentic scale speaks of improvement in the singular and in the individual—often, indeed, related to him/herself—whereas the member who scores high on the Communal scale speaks of improvement as related to "the society," "the nation," or "all people."

Those who sound the Communal theme say it is true for them that "God is found more in community and relationship than in individual lives." But high-scoring Communals react quite differently to the statement that "wealth is a sign of God's favor." They not only met it with a firm negative, but some of them, on hearing the statement read, laughed aloud.

Focus: Vertical–Horizontal

VERTICAL

Set your troubled hearts at rest. Trust in God always; trust also in me. There are many dwelling-places in my Father's house; if it were not so I should have told you; for I am going there on purpose to prepare a place for you.

John 14:1–2

HORIZONTAL

Then the righteous will reply, "Lord, when was it that we saw you hungry and fed you, or thirsty and gave you drink, a stranger and took you home, or naked and clothed you? When did we see you ill or in prison, and come to visit you?" And the king will answer, "I tell you this: anything you did for one of my brothers here, however humble, you did for me."

Matthew 25:37–40

The Vertical and the Horizontal themes deal with the tendency of people to see their religion as directing their attention principally to the relationship between God and the individual (Vertical) or to the relationship between themselves and other persons (Horizontal).

Much conflict in the history of the church, and much present-day dissension within thousands of local congregations, is traceable to differences in the emphasis that members active in policy making and church governance put on either the Vertical or the Horizontal theme. Some mainline churches, looking back on their own recent history, are dealing with the rueful suspicion that they seriously neglected Vertical concerns during the late sixties and early seventies, in favor of concentrating on Horizontal concerns—working for justice for blacks and the poor, in trying to influence public policy on a number of social issues. And in slipping out of touch with their Vertical orientation, they found that their activity placed too heavy reliance on the strong-arm methods and win-at-all-costs motivations of those whose stands they opposed.

The monastic movement, concentration on prayer, reverence in worship, practice of meditation and contemplation, concentrating on a concern for knowing God, experiencing the presence of God—all are Vertically oriented. Sermons on ethical concerns; exhorting people to love one another, to show compassion and concern; seeking justice for the oppressed; the setting up and support of social agencies, whether church-sponsored or community-sponsored—these are all Horizontally oriented.

The central symbol of the Christian church, the cross, is frequently used to symbolize these two themes—the upright of the cross symbolizing the Vertical individual-to-God relationship and the crossbar symbolizing the Horizontal person-to-person relationship. The orthodox Christian message customarily delivered is that one does not have the cross—that is, the full message that Christianity is intended to deliver—unless one focuses attention on *both* relationship with God and relationship with others.

The Vertical Theme in the Congressional Interview

The Vertical theme places high value on maintaining a firm relationship with God. Those with high Vertical scores report engaging in prayer every day, some of them several times a day. They also say that they have at some time experienced having specific prayers answered. When asked what their religious beliefs and convictions tell them concerning how to lead their lives, members who play the Vertical theme usually mention evangelizing—telling others about the influence of God in their own lives. They may also say that their religion encourages them to nurture and strengthen their own spiritual lives. Coder ratings of members on a continuum marked Vertical-high to Vertical-low find that members who were rated as high Vertical show the other characteristics of the Vertical theme as well.

The Horizontal (Justice) Theme in the Congressional Interview

Members achieved high scores on the Horizontal theme by expressing eagerness to see that everyone gets a fair chance in life. In response to a question about what one's religious beliefs and convictions say about how one should lead one's life, members who scored high said that their religious beliefs urge them to seek justice for the helpless, to help the oppressed, or to work for peace. Though they may mention other effects religious belief has on their lives, justice for the oppressed takes priority. In response to a question asked earlier in the interview about what difference their faith makes in their life—how, if at all, they are different from what they would otherwise be—the people who sounded this theme said that their faith urges them to seek justice for all, to be concerned about others, even people whom they do not know or will never see. Global concerns— concern for world peace and interest in improving the social and economic condition of all humanity—are strong for these people. The coder rating on high Horizontal to low Horizontal placed these people at the high end of the scale.

Message Received: Restricting–Releasing

RESTRICTING

O Lord, who may lodge in thy tabernacle?
Who may dwell on thy holy mountain?
The man of blameless life, who does what is right
and speaks the truth from his heart;
who has no malice on his tongue,
who never wrongs a friend
and tells no tales against his neighbour.

Psalm 15:1–3

RELEASING

I am the door; anyone who comes into the fold through me shall be safe. He shall go in and out and shall find pasturage. The thief comes only to steal, to kill, to destroy; I have come that men may have life, and may have it in all its fullness.

John 10:9–10

What do people think their religion tells them about how to approach life? Is the main message one of control, discipline, restraint, self-control, limits, and boundaries? Or is it one that makes the person feel liberated, enabled to speak and act without undue concern for transgressing limits or for risking others' disapproval? Does religion restrict me, telling me to draw back, avoid temptation, obey the rules and laws, stay out of trouble? Or does it release me to live up to and beyond my capacity because I rely principally on the strength and approval of God? Support for both messages is easy to find in Scripture. For the Restricting message the Ten Commandments offer ready examples. The Commandments are clearly a set of guidelines, more of them beginning "you shall not" than beginning "you shall," and all ten set forth standards. On the Releasing side there are many of Jesus' words. "I am the light of the world. No follower of mine shall wander in the dark; he shall have the light of life.... You shall know the truth, and the truth will set you free.... If the Son sets you free, you will indeed be free." (John 8:12, John 8:31–36, NEB.)

In the best-regulated life script the Restricting theme is perhaps played rather loudly at the beginning. In adolescence the young person, oversensitive to the restrictive side of religion, may insist on playing the Releasing theme more loudly than parents would like. And in full maturity there is a blend, the two themes played at near-equal volume, the mature person accepting certain limits but being free within those limits.

During the congressional interview one member, taking the middle way between the Restricting and Releasing messages, took care to distinguish the term *freedom* from the word *liberty.* He identified the latter as being used more frequently by the nation's founders.

Freedom [the member said] acknowledges no boundaries; *liberty,* as the Founding Fathers used it in writing "to secure the blessings of liberty . . ." means a disciplined freedom—governing oneself according to God's law. Living within that law I am liberated from the fear of torment in the hereafter as well as from arbitrary externals in this life.

The Restricting Theme in the Congressional Interview

When members were given a list of characteristics sometimes attributed to God, units of evidence of the Restricting theme built up as the members affirmed that God is judging, strict, vindictive, and not permissive. Further units accumulated as members said that their religion is related to how they live their lives in that it helps them determine limits, shapes their conscience, persuades them to avoid certain kinds of behavior. The difference that religion makes in their lives was described as self-restraint and self-control. Another unit contributing to the Restricting theme was the definition of the path to salvation as virtuous living, obedience to God, or the avoidance of evil. Another unit was a coder rating on a continuum between rigidity and flexibility which placed the member toward the rigid end, and on a law-gospel continuum (*law* being rules and standards as the major guide for life, and *gospel* being interpreted as love and forgiveness as the major guide for life) which placed the member at the law-oriented end.

Another element contributing to the Restricting theme was the statement that there is one religion that is truer than all others. This view echoes the religiously fundamental view that truth can be located, known, identified, and separated from all other views.

Members of Congress who showed a high degree of the Restricting theme said things like this:

The teaching of Christ gives us a basis ... for the formation of our patterns, morals, and ethics.

I look upon religion as imposing proper discipline on people.... I like to feel the compulsion of periodic church attendance and certain rules, certain requirements, certain conditions that I am supposed to meet. The discipline of it has validity.

In my life religious faith is a constant reminder for me to keep making that determination of what is right and what is wrong.... For example, in Congress, whether you want to press the law to its extreme so that you can get by, or whether you want to keep a cushion between you and what is not acceptable....

The path to salvation is to believe in God and follow his precepts, which are the Ten Commandments, basically.

My religion makes all the difference in the world. I am deterred from doing some things, motivated to do others. It is a controlling force in my life.

The Releasing Theme in the Congressional Interview

Unlike those who play the Restricting theme, those who play the Releasing theme experience religion as a liberating element in their lives. They believe that God accepts them just as they are and that they are forgiven. They say they feel set free from guilt over the past or from being bound by the fear of what people might say. There are enough overtones of the sturdy self-concept in this theme to raise the question of whether what we detect is a psychological set rather than the reflection of a particular religious theme. Or perhaps the two are not separate. However, the sense of freedom seems connected in the member's mind with religious belief. Another unit that contributes to a high score on Releasing is the judgment of coders and interviewers that the member is near the "liberating" end of a continuum that ran from religion-as-liberating to religion-as-restricting.

Consequence: Comfort–Challenge

COMFORT

Hear me O God, hear my lament; keep me safe from the threats of the enemy.
Hide me from the factions of the wicked,
from the turbulent mob of evildoers, who sharpen their tongues like swords . . .

Psalm 64:1–3

Come to me, all whose work is hard, whose load is heavy; and I will give you relief.

Matthew 11:28

CHALLENGE

You must not think that I have come to bring peace to the earth; I have not come to bring peace, but a sword. I have come to set a man against his father, a daughter against her mother, a son's wife against her mother-in-law; and a man will find his enemies under his own roof.

Matthew 10:34–36

According to the adage, religion has two effects on individuals: it comforts the afflicted and it afflicts the comfortable. Most people find it difficult to receive the two messages in appropriate proportions. Many have a regrettable tendency, no matter how comfortable they may be, to seek further comforts and avoid the challenges their religion offers. Ask in any church or synagogue about the number who turn up for the social event versus the number who volunteer for any kind of social service. There are many who turn to religion for comfort and solace from the pains and tensions of life, but who turn a deaf ear to the equally strong word that religion, when taken with full seriousness, should alter their lives in some way. The gospel hymns of the late 1800s resound with the Comfort theme: "Safe in the arms of Jesus." "Rock of Ages, cleft for me; let me hide myself in Thee." Some of the favorite Scripture passages of all time relate to comfort: "The Lord is my Shepherd; I shall not want . . ." No one would deny that there is a universal need for support and comfort in what is often a cold and demanding world. Comfort is a perfectly appropriate benefit to be realized from one's religious convictions. But a balanced view of religion will not focus on Comfort to the exclusion of Challenge. The charge that religion, once institutionalized, has a tendency to overplay the Comfort theme has been made by figures as diverse as Karl Marx and Jesus of Nazareth.

The Comfort Theme in the Congressional Interview

The Comfort theme made itself heard from three sources. Two of them came from observations of both interviewers and coders, placing the interviewee on a Comfort-Challenge continuum. In ways not related directly to specific questions, it came clear to those who heard the interview that this person derived comfort from his or her religious beliefs. The third source tells how heavily the member emphasized statements about the contribution of his/her religious belief to comfort, strength, courage, power, positive outlook, assurance, and meaning in life. Special attention was given to whether these elements were emphasized above all others mentioned in response to the question, What difference, if any, does your religious faith make in your life? In other words, one did not receive a high Comfort score merely by mentioning that one's faith was a source of strength; high Comfort scores went to those who said that religion was a source of strength and who *also* said nothing about the influence of religion on concern for justice, self-control, interpersonal relationships, high ethical standards, or other more challenging consequences of religious faith.

The Challenge Theme in the Congressional Interview

The Challenge theme sounds the note that religion ought to inspire its adherents to be up and doing. What they ought to be doing is not explicit in the interview measure; it simply makes clear that an armchair religion, a religion that stays inside the mind and heart of a person, isn't sufficient. Religion should be translated into action of some sort. It should move one toward better citizenship, toward service of some kind to others, toward being more loving, toward working for peace or justice, toward higher ethical standards, toward sensitivity to the needs of others, toward being a good example, toward being a productive worker, toward being a good parent, toward being dedicated to country. All of these were mentioned by members during the interview; what binds them together is not the area toward which the effort should be directed, but that they think religion should challenge people toward some kind of perceptible change. In the biblical phrase, "By their fruits you shall know them." Those who sound the Challenge theme believe that religious beliefs should result in changed behavior.

Importance Scales and Theological Emphases

The next scale descriptions concern the remaining five, more familiar ways of describing religious positions. The first three deal with *basic theological orientation* and the last two with *importance* of religion and the institutional church.

Evangelicals

The Evangelical theme emphasizes the nearness of God. Members sound this theme by showing that they feel their faith deeply and personally. The images of God that come most quickly to their minds are the loving, close, parental images of God: God is a dependable companion and friend who gives guidance, direction, and comfort. They believe that God has a plan for their lives and believe it is part of their continuing task to try to discern that plan and follow it.

Their images of Jesus are similar to their images of God.

Jesus is personal savior, companion, friend, and guide. The path to salvation in the Evangelical theme is not so much in doing as in believing; salvation comes through belief in God or faith in and acceptance of Christ's sacrifice for humanity.

One unit of the Evangelical theme declares that everything presented in Scripture is true and factual. Other contributing units are having had an identifiable experience of being born again and having had the experience of feeling God's presence.

Christian Orthodoxy

Orthodoxy is a term that has been used for centuries and carefully defined numerous times in numerous ways. No one, so far as we know, has developed a reliable way of measuring it. Perhaps it has not been thought necessary to develop a test of orthodoxy, since many theologians think they can spot it unaided. The units that came together to serve as an Orthodoxy scale formed by themselves—because of the way members responded to the questions—out of a possible set of 124 items. When these units are set out in list form, they sound rather surprisingly like a test of willingness to repeat the Apostles' Creed (although they omit reference to the Trinity, since the interview lacked that concept). There are five elements, which we have named Christian Orthodoxy, that arose from the congressional interviews because of a particular consistency in the way members responded to them. They are:

1. Belief that God is a personal Being who has feelings, consciousness, and a will
2. Belief that Jesus was divine
3. Belief in the reality of life after death
4. Belief in the existence of both heaven and hell
5. Belief that God played a role in the writing of Scripture

The Orthodoxy scale is taken as a measure of willingness to accept the basic tenets of faith common to most Christian groups.

Symbolic God

A minority of members describe God as an awesome, vast, mysterious presence that will never be clearly knowable by hu-

man beings—something almost entirely outside and beyond human understanding. Whereas Orthodox Christians tend to affirm that God is a being with feeling, consciousness, and will,
the Symbolic God theme understands God as force, order, process, spirit. Close, personal terms like *friend, companion,* and
helper almost never occur in the conversation of one who understands God as Symbolic. Nor would such a person choose terms
that convey a standard-setting relationship—God as demanding, stern, or judging. In spite of the relatively impersonal
terms in which they describe God, members who sound the
Symbolic theme do not necessarily believe God to be entirely
removed from human contact or understanding. Some believe
that God may be evolving and changing throughout the course
of history.

A God too awesome to be captured in everyday language, a
God difficult to grasp, a God operating at a very high level of
abstraction and complexity is the God of the Symbolic God
theme.

Pro-Church

Pro-Church members of Congress do not have to introduce
themselves to their pastor or priest when they appear on Sunday morning. They report frequent church attendance and can
name a number of specific church leadership roles that they
have taken in the past or are now taking. Besides these behavioral self-reports they demonstrate attitudes favorable to the institutional church. They rejected a question that invited them to
say that the church often inhibits the development of mature
religious faith, and affirmed the statement that they had come
to know God better through the church. Having lived through
a time when it was reasonably fashionable among the well-edu-
cated to have given up on the institutional church, Pro-Church
members have held on to their belief in the identity of the
church as the body of Christ and in its value as a positive force
in their own lives.

Pro-Religion

Being Pro-Church and being Pro-Religion are not quite the
same thing. A small set—three scores from the interview—

emerged to offer a measure of how important religion is to each of the persons interviewed. The first score is composed of an observation of the certainty with which the member spoke about the identify of God, and the emphasis placed on each of the attributes of God mentioned. A second came from the coders' judgment about whether religion was central or peripheral to this member's life and consciousness. Toward the end of the interview the member was asked to talk about how important religion had been throughout her/his personal history, and then to declare how important it now is. The third score was derived from the member's estimate of religion's current importance. (A reminder: Coders did not hear or read the final part of the interview in which the member declared the present importance of religion; the coders' judgment of the importance of religion to the member was made independent of the member's own statement.)

Mixtures of Themes

We make no claim to have isolated everything there is to discover about how religion is manifested in people's lives and what part it plays in their thought and action. But we have discovered a great deal; these themes play large parts in everyone's religious identity. Yet, near-infinite variety is present among us, according to the mixture and intensities with which these themes are alive and working in us. In addition, variation occurs not only between the theme-patterns of individuals, but within the same person at different times, in different environments, and at different points in the religious journey. Knowledge of the themes simply helps to describe those elements as they are at work in us.

Each of us probably incorporates some measure of all thirteen themes. Even the eight that seem like opposites can coexist in equally high degrees in some persons.[5] For example, some demonstrate the Restricting theme by willingly adopting in their personal lives some very rigid disciplines—a vow of poverty, for instance. Yet these same people, freed of the worries that burden most of us, often emerge as serenely courageous, risk-taking leaders, clearly illustrating the Releasing theme.

Portraits of Six Religious Types

All that has preceded in this chapter is prologue to the portraits we now begin to draw. The themes just described are useful in that they summarize some of the common tendencies of religious people. We now know that there are objectively identifiable, predictable things people say about their religious beliefs and behavior that serve as reliable indicators of the degree to which those themes are present in their lives.

The focus of this chapter, however, is on the six distinct types of religious belief represented in the Congress. (See table 8-1.) These six were discovered by statistical means, in which we used a sophisticated analytical technique called *cluster analysis* to allow members to fall into different types, based on how they scored on the thirteen scales.[6] Our research locates and describes them as they exist in Congress, but their average-citizen counterparts can likely be found in every community in the nation. In the descriptions of the types of congressional religionists that follow, one will no doubt see images of real people marching across the pages—images of people with whom, or against whom, one has contended in many a weary churchly or political battle.

These are the six types and the percentages of Congress that fall into each type:

Legalistic religionists—15 percent
Integrated religionists—14 percent
Self-Concerned religionists—29 percent
People-Concerned religionists—10 percent
Nontraditional religionists—9 percent
Nominal religionists—22 percent

The first four of these fall into one group, the last two into a second. The first four show considerable similarity on several of the scales. They are either moderate or high on Christian Orthodoxy, Evangelical, Pro-Church, and Pro-Religion. In other words, members of all of these groups would probably be observed to attend church with some regularity, to speak well of the role of the church in society, to acknowledge that religion has personal importance to her/him, and, at least when the sub-

Table 8-1. Six Religious Types in the United States Congress

	Legalistic Religionists	Self-Concerned Religionists	Integrated Religionists	People-Concerned Religionists	Non-Traditional Religionists	Nominal Religionists
Percentage of Congressional Sample	15%	29%	14%	10%	9%	22%
Dominant Religious Themes						
Agentic–Communal	High Agentic	High Agentic	Moderate or high on both	High Communal	High Communal	
Vertical–Horizontal		High Vertical	Moderate or high on both	High Horizontal	High Horizontal	
Comforting–Challenging		High Comforting	Moderate or high on both	High Challenge		High Comforting
Restricting–Releasing	High Restricting		Moderate or high on both	High Releasing		

Theological Orientation					
Christian Orthodoxy	High	High	High	Moderate	Low	Low
Evangelical	Moderate	High	Moderate *	Moderate	Low	Low
Symbolic	Moderate	Low	Low	Low	High	High
Importance					
Pro-Church	Moderate	High	High	Moderate	Low	Low
Pro-Religion	Moderate	High	High	High	Moderate	Low
Distinguishing God-images	Personal, strict, judging	Personal, companion, friend	Personal, loving, caring	Personal, freeing, liberating	God as abstract, nonpersonal	Aloof, distant, impersonal
Value Emphases	Self-restraint	Traditional values	Love	Justice	Justice	(Low on all value orientations)

ject is raised, to be able to talk knowledgeably, positively, and with some warmth about the attributes of God, the character of Jesus Christ, the power of prayer, and the existence of life after death. People who know them would probably consider all of these to be good, religious folk, positive to and supportive of religion and the church. Because of their similarity on these observable phenomena, it would be easy to assume that their similarities go further, extending to similarities in the way they receive, understand, feel, and act out the consequences of their religious faith.

Nothing could be further from the truth. They constitute *four distinct groups* who begin to be visibly different from one another as soon as we examine their locations on the eight *religious theme* scores. (Charts showing the location of the scores of each type on the eight religious themes are given in appendix B.)

The Legalistic Religionists

Rules, laws, guidelines for behavior, spoken and unspoken agreements adhered to, contracts, promises—all of these are necessary to a livable environment. Sunrise and sunset; fall, winter, spring, summer; "Right turn on red permitted"; "Black tie only, please"; "The undersigned promises to pay . . ."—all of these form a climate in which we can make individual judgments and decisions, knowing that there are certain things on which we can count as points of reference. Whether the laws are informal agreements, human laws, or the laws of God, we depend on them to form a framework in which we can move about with a certain degree of assurance for ourselves and a certain degree of trust in others.

Members of Congress whom we identify as Legalistic religionists place very high value on rules, boundaries, limits, guidelines, direction, and purpose. This element enters repeatedly into the interview statements. Ask them about God, and their images of God depict God as lawgiver. Ask them what difference their religion makes in their lives, and their primary response is that it imposes a discipline on them, causes them to be more circumspect, more self-restrained than they otherwise might be. Ask them about the solution to the major human problem and they respond by saying, "Direction and purpose for life." The religion of the Legalists serves as a cosmic anchor, a source of stability. It represents dependability, certainty, and solidity in a shifting and ambiguous world.

The 15 percent of the congressional sample who occupy the Legalistic position scored higher than any other group on two of the eight themes: Agentic and Restricting. Their high score on Restricting, head and shoulders above the score of any other group, is given further emphasis by the fact that they scored, as a group, *lower* than any other on Restricting's logical opposite, the Releasing scale.

When members of this group were asked what differences religion makes in their lives, 81 percent of everything they said was related to guidance, discipline, and self-restraint. With the exception of the Self-Concerned religionists, whose mention of guidance and self-restraint made up 38 percent of their responses, in every other group fewer than 8 percent of the answers included self-restraint language.

From the list of twenty-one characteristics outlining God-images, the Legalists placed more emphasis than other types on "strict," "aware of everything I think and do," "judging," and "knowable."

One of several subjective judgments coders were asked to make at the end of each interview-coding session was to give a rating on a continuum between examined and unexamined. A person with an examined set of religious beliefs would have given evidence that he/she had done a good deal of soul-searching, had tested belief against reality, and had not swallowed whole every doctrinal statement set out by that member's church or other spiritual authority. On the examined-unexamined continuum the average rank for the Legalistic group shares the lowest rating (indicating a relatively unexamined set of beliefs) with the Nominal Religionists. Legalistic religionists prize rules and guidelines to such an extent, apparently, that they give little evidence of having tested the religious guidelines with which they have been presented. Like a climber fearing to test the belay rope lest it be found unsafe, the Legalist prefers to trust rather than test the doctrinal equipment issued for the lifelong journey.

The Self-Concerned Religionists

About a third of our congressional sample espouse a religious faith that is devoted, visible, articulate, enthusiastically shared, regularly practiced, apparently genuine—and almost entirely concerned with the relationship between the believer and God. The belief pattern of the Self-Concerned religionist includes relatively little impetus toward concern for fellow creatures.

Members of this group are likely to appear to those around them to be "more religious" than any other group. They score higher than any other group on these four scales: Pro-Religion, Pro-Church, Christian Orthodoxy, and Evangelical.

On the eight *religious theme* scales what distinguishes them are two very high scores: a score that is markedly higher than any other group on the Vertical theme (the close-relationship-with-God theme) and a score higher than any other on the Comfort theme. They speak with feeling about the comfort and solace they derive from their religious beliefs. "There's a feeling of great assurance," says one member. ". . . I've been in danger—physical danger—and . . . I had some sense of security from God, from a Supreme Being." "God is, to me," says another member, "somebody who gives me times of strength, good feelings, and warmth when I'm in need. . . . I find it difficult to put in conceptual terms."

The Self-Concerned average score on the Agentic theme is the second highest among all groups; in a population as filled with Agentic movers and shakers as Congress, such a high Agentic score spells considerable devotion to the personal-action, self-oriented way of viewing life. At the other end of the ranking, the Self-Concerned have the lowest score on the Communal scale (the scale indicating the perception of unity and interdependence).

There are a number of similarities between the Legalists and the Self-Concerned. The two rank first and second on the Agentic and Restricting themes. They rank last and next to last on the Communal and Releasing themes—the two that are logical opposites of Agentic and Restricting. Both types prefer clear limits, firm guidelines, goal-directed activity, and strict discipline. They present a clearly recognizable image.

Throughout our study we have continued to ask the chicken-egg question, Do these people adopt religious positions because of a certain psychological set that makes a clear-limits religion most acceptable, or is the religious position the impetus for the development of a matching psychological set? We have no answer for the question. However, since these two differ in the degree to which they seem to value church membership, certain common religious doctrines, and religion in general, the Self-Concerned would tend to reinforce the religious etiology theory, and the Legalists would reinforce the psychological etiology theory.

The Integrated Religionists

The distinguishing mark of the Integrated religionists is their higher-than-all-others rank on the Releasing theme. These people's religious beliefs work to liberate, to free them to speak and act. In the familiar phrase, God, not humankind, is their audience. When hard choices must be made, Integrated religionists can put aside the all-too-human desire—intensified, we are led to believe, in politicans—to please people (read "the voting public") in favor of a choice that is less popular but that is in accordance with their conscience, their understanding of God's intention.

Integrated religionists present a portrait that shows them balancing between the extremes on several pairs of themes, able much of the time to be "both-and" rather than "either-or." They are both Agentic and Communal, with moderate scores on both scales, but with the Communal score higher. They take next-to-highest rank on the Vertical and moderate on the Horizontal theme. Although they rank highest of all on the Releasing theme, they are in a moderate position on the Restricting theme—a position that acknowledges their desire for guidelines and discipline even in the midst of freedom.

At first glance the profile of the Integrated religionists bears some similarity to the profile of the Nominal religionists. The average scores of both tend toward the middle on several of the thirteen themes. But there is a great difference in the way the beliefs of the two types are held and in the way they are expressed. That difference will be discussed later, when the

Nominal religionists are described. However, one difference is worth mentioning here. One important difference between them shows in the coders' ratings on the examined-unexamined continuum. Whereas the Nominalists share bottom ratings (closest to unexamined) with the Legalists, the Integrated religionists share the top-rated spot (closest to examined) with the People-Concerned religionists. Integrated religionists have tested their faith against life, while Nominalists don't appear to have taken the trouble.

The People-Concerned Religionists

The fourth religious type comprises a small but important segment of Congress. The People-Concerned group received top scores on three themes, and these themes present a well-defined image.

The People-Concerned religionists score markedly higher than any other group on both the Challenge and the Horizontal themes. On Horizontal, the average score is so high that it almost flies off the edge of the chart. This 10 percent of the members of Congress believe intensely that religious belief ought to move one to action (hence the very high Challenge score) and that an important focus of that action should be on responding to the needs of the oppressed and the have-nots of world (hence the very high Horizontal score).

In addition to their extremely high Challenge and Horizontal scores, the People-Concerned have a score on the Communal theme that is higher than that of any other group. This score is paired with a relatively low Agentic score.

The People-Concerned group is first cousin to the Integrated religionists. On the Pro-Church and Pro-Religion scales they occupy almost exactly the same positions; the practice of their religion is important to both groups, and both groups appreciate and are involved in church life. On the Evangelical theme the Integrated and the People-Concerned are very nearly at the same place, on the high side of moderate. The two groups are also similar in that they experience religion as more Releasing than Restricting. For neither group is the Comfort of religious belief very much emphasized.

The People-Concerned group is remarkable for its members'

refusal to settle for easy definitions of the nature of God, though they also gave enough evidence of a sufficiently traditional set of beliefs that they received a moderate Christian Orthodoxy score. In responding to the question, Is God a being with feelings, consciousness, and will, or is God something else? they did not quite reject the statement, but added other things around it, such as:

God is a personality. . . . I'm not sure I could handle God other than as an abstract idea without the incarnation. . . . Without that, God would have been impersonal, aloof, withdrawn, . . . except for the incarnation.

Well, the only thing I don't like about that is the personalization. . . . You can fall into a trap, personalizing God, identifying God in human semblance.

Well, first of all, I don't think of God as a man. I think of God as a verb. . . . I'm one of those who want to move away from the patriarchal, hierarchal concept of God and religion.

Well, I don't think God is a personal being who can be described in anthropomorphic terms. I think those terms are inadequate. . . . *Knowing* I can accept, but not *being*. . . . A *knowing* that has a broader design in history and human lives; omniscient, omnipotent, all-powerful, quick to forgive. . . .

It is easy on reading these responses to see why this group, along with the Integrated religionists, received the highest score on examined religion. The language used and the concepts expressed are those of people who aren't still living on their childhood instruction in religion; they've traveled many a long mile of experience and learning since those days. In these people's conversation one hears names like Tillich, Bultmann, Niebuhr, and Teilhard de Chardin. They have read current thought in the field of religion. They have thought about it; no doubt they have argued about it. And the net effect of this active pursuit of the meaning and nature of religious belief is to move these people to a strong concern for others, for seeing that justice is available for the weak as well as for the strong. At least two in this group attributed their decision to run for Congress to a religion-related concern for others.

There is a curious combination of energy and calm that is

communicated through the interviews with these people. The calm, to be fair, may have been a result of their relative comfort with the topics being explored. But there is also an energy, an enthusiasm for the possibility of change in the country and the world that gives their interviews a unique, hopeful flavor.

The Nontraditional Religionists

The distinguishing characteristic of this 9 percent of our congressional sample is that its members have a markedly higher average rating on the Symbolic God theme than any of the other groups. Their God is abstract, not so much a personal being as a force, spirit, or some other concept that they can't quite describe. Nontraditionalists are alike in that they are sturdily intellectually honest; they refuse to take the convenient, socially acceptable way of lightly accepting any of the standard descriptions of God. They struggle toward a description that they know in advance they cannot fully articulate. As was true of the People-Concerned, the question of the identity of God has importance for this group, and they are not willing to deal with it in a superficial way. Nevertheless, they are not all alike. One of their number, while affirming a distant, abstract God, also related a vivid personal experience that he firmly believes was an encounter with the power of God. He acknowledged the contradiction between his story and his general belief but was not willing to forsake his concept of a Symbolic God to fit that one memorable experience.

Illustration of some of the ways in which the Nontraditional religionists speak about Religious Reality may help to make their positions more understandable.

[*Interviewer:* Were you ever a believer, a firm believer in a supernatural reality at any point in your life?] No. I've never affirmatively believed in a supernatural being. I've never discounted the possibility of it, but never affirmatively accepted.... [If I had proof] I'd be delighted to.

I believe in a Supreme Being or Supreme Force that at least initiated this universe and the world in which we live. It is a force larger than human beings and created both the universe in which the world exists and the world in which we live.

[*Interviewer:* Is God a personal being that has feelings, consciousness, and will, or is God something else?] I would think he's something else. It has a lot to do with how one views him. I don't think that God actually appears to all of these people that claim they've talked to God.

[*Interviewer:* Would you say God has knowledge and acts?] Well, I would think in a broad sense that he acts. I don't think he dictates individual actions to humans, but I think he has set out some broad parameters for us to stay within. I think of a God that's fair and just. I think one ought to love God.

The great problem is that I think that sometimes I've had some experience of some outside Being comforting me. And yet, you look at the world, you can't blame God for all the misery and wars and everything. If you say, "Is it God's will that the Indians starve?" that doesn't make any sense to me. [*Interviewer:* Are there terms that describe that Being?] I guess it's a source of personal strength or encouragement. [Member relates personal story.] And so that's why I could never just say there isn't some Being that in some way you can get some strength from, and yet, you know. . . .

Their God differs from the God of the Nominalists (who rank next highest on the Symbolic God theme) in that the God of the Nontraditionalists is a relatively permissive God; the Nontraditional religionists' concept of God does not have the Nominalists' note of a strict, direction-giving God.

There is a remarkable lack of balance between the pairs of religious themes for the Nontraditionals; this lack of balance is probably the greatest distinguishing feature of this type. There is a wide gap between a very low Agentic score and a high Communal score. The gap is even wider between the low Vertical and high Horizontal scores. The gap between Comfort and Challenge is marked, but not as wide as the first two mentioned. The only pair of themes that comes within hailing distance of being balanced for Nontraditionals is the Restricting and Releasing scores—and even there the gap is noticeable.

On 7 of the thirteen themes this group occupies the lowest rank. They are lowest Agentic, lowest Vertical, lowest Restricting, lowest Comfort, lowest Pro-Church, lowest Evangelical, and lowest Christian Orthodoxy.

The Nontraditionals' lowest-of-all rank on the Vertical theme makes sense, coming along with a high Symbolic God score. If God is not a being, but a force, spirit, or process, one is less likely to believe God reachable by any human effort. The Vertical score might be called a contact-with-God score, since it arises mostly from interviewees' statements about frequency of prayer and the experience of answers to prayer. One who believes in a distant, inaccessible God is not likely to initiate the kind of contact—prayer—common to those who believe God is accessible.

The lowest rank on Comfort also fits the high Symbolic, low Vertical pattern. Believing that God is not involved in day-to-day contact with human beings, Nontraditionalists do not live with the kind of comfort and assurance enjoyed by those who perceive God as close, companionable, and reassuring.

Paired with the low Vertical score is a high Horizontal score. The direction in which the Nontraditionalists' religion mediates is toward the Communal and toward the Horizontal—toward concern for and activity on behalf of one's fellow human beings. If one's religious thinking consists of more questions than certainties about God (or Religious Reality), then one focuses instead on people. If one is not sure about immortality, the effect one has on the shape of this present life gathers increased importance. Social justice and the welfare of one's fellow humans is of great interest to this group.

Paired with the Nontraditionalists' low Agentic score is a high Communal score. For all practical purposes the group is tied for top rank with the People-Concerned group.

If there is a single group whose public statements and stands have given rise to the secular-humanism charge against Congress, it is probably this group. They are the people least likely to fit quietly into someone else's religious categories, especially if the categories are religiously fundamental in tone. They will not settle for easy definitions or imprecise distinctions. However, we did not find between this 9 percent and other members the gap of belief in a transcendent Religious Reality that we might have anticipated in hearing the charges regularly leveled at Congress. They seem as dedicated and concerned as many another more evangelically inclined legislator; coders rated them as possessing a more vital set of beliefs, as a group, than either the highly evangelical Self Concerned or the Legalists.

The Nominal Religionists

We may as well get it said first as last; the scriptural text keeps running like a refrain through our heads as we consider this group. "I know all your ways; you are neither hot nor cold" (Rev. 3:15).

This group shows relatively little enthusiasm for most of the religious themes. On seven of the thirteen themes they rank last or next to last. They show a modest interest in two themes: the Comfort theme (religion that offers solace in time of need) and the Symbolic God theme (God as a distant, impersonal, removed, abstract figure). However, on even their highest scores they do not get beyond the moderate category.

If any group comes under suspicion of maintaining church membership as a social or political expedient rather than as a personal declaration of faith, it is this group, which comprises about 22 percent of the congressional sample. They rank lowest of all on Pro-Religion and next to lowest on the Pro-Church theme. On the lifeline question, where each interviewee estimated the depth of personal commitment to religious faith at various points in life, this group gave the lowest average self-estimate.

However, anyone familiar with religious institutional life knows that there are members of most congregations who have a similarly lukewarm relationship with the church and religion. There is a segment of the American public to whom it seems desirable to keep in touch with the church, as long as one doesn't get too enthusiastic about it or make any major commitments. This segment of Congress may simply be representative of that position. Political considerations may play little, if any, part.

The other theme (besides Pro-Religion) on which this group ranks markedly lower than others is Challenge. In the Comfort– Challenge pair, Comfort is a runaway winner. This group does not sense a strong push for personal change of any sort emanating from their religious beliefs; the lack is not surprising, since their religious beliefs are in themselves rather loosely held. On both the Vertical and the Horizontal themes—both relationship with God and concern for social change as a religious value—Nominal religionists rank next to last.

Coders, asked to rank all interviewees on a continuum between religion as central to the person or peripheral, rated the religious beliefs of this group to be most nearly peripheral—more than one full point, on a seven-point scale, lower than any other group.

Similarly, on the examined-unexamined continuum, coders gave the lowest average rating (indicating a relatively unexamined set of beliefs) to this group—a rating very similar to that of the Legalistic religionists.

A cursory look at the profiles of Integrated religionists and Nominalists might cause one to believe that there is a similarity between them. Both the similarities and the differences become evident in the following quotations from some of the congressional interviews.

Some similarity between a Nominal and an Integrated appears in these two responses to a question about the identity of Jesus.

Nominal: Jesus is—in the Christian religion—the Son of God, and I think he is an inspirational figure who certainly was one of the most influential persons in history, and . . .' [long pause] I think he was quasi-supernatural, but I'm not sure of the rising from the dead and all of that. I don't have a strong belief in that.

Integrated: Jesus, I think, was a divinely inspired person. I don't believe he was divine in the sense that the church generally accepts it.

Both have intellectually examined the question of the divinity of Jesus, and the two would seem to have come to about the same conclusion, although we cannot be sure what the Integrated member means by "in the sense that the church generally accepts."

However, another Integrated affirms the divinity of Jesus in this relatively orthodox way:

Integrated: Jesus is the Son of God. He's also a part of God. He's part of the Trinity. They all combine to make the concept.

The differences between Nominalists and Integrated religionists are more clear in this pair of responses to the question, What would you say is the difference your religious beliefs have made in your life?

Nominalist: Oh, there was a difference when I was younger. Less now. I think what helps us is the religious atmosphere: knowing that my parents did things that gave me direction by example. And I want to do that for my children.

Integrated: I think I am in public service because of a profound belief ... in the purpose for which God has put us here. I think my belief in God dictates how I treat people and how I act myself. [Interviewer: Would you guess that, were you not to believe in God, that you would not have entered public service?] I think I would have entered public service, but with a different attitude. There are things to be gained if one wants to ... better oneself materially. I think if I did not have a profound belief in God I would behave entirely differently. . . .

The Nominalist's reply is shorter and less specific than the Integrated's. He focuses on something other than himself, and offers one of the time-honored, faintly positive statements that people advance in shamefaced explanation of their own involvement (or lack of involvement) with the institutional church: "It's a good example for the children." The Integrated, in contrast, focuses on the influence of religious belief on his own behavior.

Religion, for Nominal religionists, is all right to keep in touch with, but more for reasons of comfort than as an effective guiding force in life.

Religious Types Across Denominations

Religious types spread across denominations in quite a remarkable way. Table 8-2 presents the religious affiliations of the majority of our congressional interviewees and the number of each that fell into the six religious types.[7] Membership in a particular denomination obviously does not accurately predict the type of religionist one is. Among the Roman Catholics in our sample, at least one fell into each of the six categories. The same is true for members of the mainline Protestant churches.

The other three groups, probably because they are represented by smaller numbers, miss being represented in one or two categories.

Members of Congress are an unusual group (for example, they are more highly educated, more personally assertive, and more preponderantly male than the general population), and the way they fall into the six categories may be unique. Furthermore, it is unsound to generalize from the way groups as small as these (ranging in number from four members to thirty) find membership in six categories. However, the point is well illustrated: knowing a legislator's denomination does not tell us very much about his or her religious beliefs.

Table 8-2. Religious Affiliation and the Six Religious Types

	Legalistic	Self-Concerned	Integrated	People-Concerned	Non-Traditional	Nominal	Total*
Catholic	3	3	4	1	1	4	16
Liberal Protestant	1	3	0	1	2	4	11
Mainline Protestant	4	12	4	3	2	5	30
Conservative Protestant	2	2	3	2	0	2	11
Jewish	1	0	0	1	2	1	5
Affiliation Unspec.	1	2	0	0	0	1	4

*The total number of members included in the cluster analyses was seventy-seven. Three members had missing data on one or more of the 13 variables, and therefore could not be included.

The figures in table 8-2 help explain why earlier researchers, studying the political stance of members of Congress by organizing members according to denomination, could not achieve meaningful results. Knowing a legislator's denomination may tell you something about the type of message delivered to members by that church, but it does not tell how the message is received and translated into the legislator's understandings and religious attitudes.

A caution: One should not generalize the information above to denominations as a whole. It would not be safe to assume that we know, for instance, the proportion of mainline Protestants in the general population who would fall into the various religious categories. Members of Congress are a select group, and the way they spread across the six types may be unique.

The six types may well be found in settings other than Congress, but in different proportions. We would not be surprised to find them existing side by side in factories, in corporate headquarters, among scientists, or on college campuses. We do not know how the distribution of this group across the types would compare with the American public or with the nation's founders. One reasonable hypothesis is that the founders, dedicated as they were to nation-building, may have had a smaller concentration in the Self-Concerned type and more in the People-Concerned.

Four of the six types—Legalist, Self-Concerned, Integrated, and People-Concerned—represent about 70 percent of the congressional sample. Members in each of these four types take religion seriously, as do some in the Nontraditional type. This corroborates the point made in chapter 4 that religion is a meaningful element of life for about three-fourths of our sample. Almost all persons (except for the few Jewish members) in these four types would call themselves Christian. But by looking at the diverse views represented in these four groups, we see that no single way of being Christian can be described. We have in the four types members who share orthodox beliefs but who differ dramatically in how they experience religion. Why these four different types of religion emerge from the same wellspring is not clear. If one's religious perspective were simply a matter of learning, we would expect persons with the same denominational background to share the same type. Since this is not the case, we have to look for other explanations. In later chapters we will consider some possibilities.

9. What Is the Connection Between Religion and Voting?

> *Myth Number Three:* Political conservatives are more religious than political liberals.
>
> *Myth Number Four:* Members' religious beliefs and values bear little relationship to how they vote on specific issues, except for a few select areas like abortion and school prayer.

- Should the federal government increase or decrease spending for the national food stamp program?
- Should the United States give foreign aid to Cambodia, Laos, and Vietnam?
- Should the federal government spend billions of dollars to develop the MX missile system?
- Should a national health program for poor children be expanded or curtailed?
- Should the federal government provide funding to help pay the cost of abortions for poor women?
- Should a tax be levied on windfall profits oil companies receive as a consequence of the lifting of oil price controls?

The questions above outline a few of the momentous decisions that confronted Congress in 1979 and 1980. They represent just a handful of the hundreds of voting decisions that face senators and representatives each year in important areas like energy, ecology, taxation, education, social welfare, foreign aid, civil rights, and military expenditures.

What forces impinge upon a member of Congress as he or she decides to vote yea or nay? Many groups, for many different reasons, want to know. Lobbyists, whose business it is to influence the members' votes, have eagerly sought insight into the principal influences. Voters want to know whether their individual voices make a difference. Political scientists have researched the question for several decades, hoping to build an explanation of the voting-behavior process. Besides lobby pressure and constituent pressure, voting-behavior explorers have looked at other factors like party platform, political ideology, and the persuasion of colleagues as possible shapers of voting choices. The most credible conclusion so far has seemed to be that there are many factors at work, and at work in some as-yet-unknown relationship to one another, the relative influence of each factor changing from issue to issue.

Throughout all this searching there has been almost no attention paid to the possible role of religious beliefs and values. The eight or ten most prominent studies of voting behavior include almost no reference to the religious dimension.[1] The few attempts to see how religious affiliation (e.g., Protestant, Catholic, Jew) relates to voting have not yielded promising results.[2] Such results are no surprise, for we noted in the previous chapter that the real differences between people, as reflected in the six types of religion, are quite independent of religious affiliation.

One major reason why theories of voting behavior have not included religion is that the necessary information about religion has not been available. One can find out easily enough what members' religious affiliations are. All one has to do is look them up in widely available resources like *The Almanac of American Politics*.[3] But when it comes to beliefs and values, there is a void. Nowhere can we find what members believe, for example, about God, or salvation, or life after death. The ties between religion and voting have not been drawn.

This project offers the first opportunity to explore and chart the ties between religion and voting. There are no studies by others to guide us or to provide a background against which we can consider our findings. The uniqueness of this venture makes it simultaneously exhilarating and frightening. There is a certain excitement in exploring new territory, and a certain anxiety about what one will find and what impact those findings will have.

What should we expect to find? The available literature and conversation with experts yielded three contradictory messages. These were:

1. Expect no relationship between religious beliefs and values and specific voting issues, except in the case of a few select topics like abortion and school prayer. Religion is one complex area of life, politics is another, and the two do not have enough in common to be related.
2. Expect religious belief to be related to political conservatism; believing members will lean toward the conservative, and less believing, less practicing members will lean toward the liberal.
3. Expect substantial and significant relationships between religion and voting. Some religious orientations will go hand in hand with a conservative political orientation, and some will go hand in hand with a liberal political orientation. Furthermore, religious beliefs and values will be strongly related to specific voting issues like civil liberties, foreign aid, military expenditures, and government spending.

We have found that the third message is most accurate. Strong ties connect religious beliefs to both general political orientation and votes that have been cast on specific issues. To set the stage for the outline of our discoveries, we begin with a brief discussion of how members themselves perceive the connection between religion and voting in their own political careers.

Religion and Voting as Members See Them

We asked each interviewee in our eighty-member sample this question: To what degree do your religious beliefs and values guide or influence your voting decisions? We acquired two different units of information from this question. One unit presents the *degree of influence* members think their religion has on voting. The other is related to the number of members who *make a conscious application* of their religious convictions to specific votes.

The following reveals what members believe about the degree of influence their religious beliefs have on their voting:

Major influence—24 percent
Moderate influence—56 percent
Minor influence—19 percent
No influence—1 percent

When we combine the top two categories, 80 percent report religion to have a perceptible influence on voting. Political liberals are as likely to say "moderate" or "major" as are conservatives; Republicans are as likely as Democrats.

We probed for an expression of their awareness of this influence. Thirty-one percent of the sample said that they were aware of a connection, reporting their own conscious effort, prior to some votes, to apply their religious principles to the voting decision. A slightly larger group, 36 percent, viewed the connection as more indirect. Since religion is a major determinant of their values and political perspectives, they said, it is likely that these values and perspectives have influenced their voting decisions, but without their being conscious of that influence.

The internal struggle that is probably familiar to many in Congress became audible in the response of one member who, though he apparently concurs with his denomination's generally antiwar stand, tends to vote for increased military expenditures. He had come to the end of his statement, saying that he thought his beliefs had some influence, especially when government could alleviate suffering. Then he added softly, as a kind of afterthought addressed mostly to himself, "I guess I just repress the military side of it completely."

Discovering the Ties Between Religion and Political Orientation

Beyond general impressions that religious belief influences voting, do we find statistical relationships between religious beliefs and political decisions? Indeed we do.

Two of the most commonly used political labels are *conserva-*

tive and *liberal.** And there are few terms more difficult to define. The difficulty is reflected by the recurring attempts of poll-takers and magazine-article writers to find the key elements that separate the two groups. In 1976 a special issue of *Commentary* asked sixty-five political scientists and other academics to respond to the questions, "What is a liberal? Who is a conservative?"[4] In August, 1980, the *New York Times Magazine* gave twenty-four pages to the question, "What is a conservative?"[5] The labels persist, the definitions multiply.

In spite of the difficulty it is possible to locate some common threads that tie conservatives together on the one hand, and liberals on the other. Political conservatives tend to favor limited government (in which the free enterprise system is protected from government interference and issues of human welfare—poverty, education, health, etc.—are left to the private sector), preserving traditional values (e.g., family, individualism, hard work), and a firm commitment to national defense. Liberals, on the other hand, tend to favor an active government which seeks to spread economic and social benefits, to change those social structures which create social "victims," and to put less emphasis on military preparedness. In the early 1980s the most dramatic conservative-liberal debates had to do with government expenditures for social programs (health care for the poor and elderly, food stamps, urban revitalization). Political conservatives see such programs as an extravagant, ineffective waste of taxpayers' money, while liberals see them as a necessary means of dealing with social problems.

Conservative/Liberal Differences in Religious Belief

Conservatives and liberals, then, have different political views. Do they also have very different religious beliefs? We gave each member a political-orientation score, using the index published by Americans for Democratic Action, a Washington-based office which rates all members' votes every year.[6] The

---

*In this chapter *conservative* and *liberal* always refer to political orientation. We will not use the terms to describe religious orientation, although we recognize that they are often so used. We will not apply them to religion, in part because we have more precisely defined terms to use, and in part to avoid the obvious potential for confusion.

index ranges from 0 to 100. The higher the score, the more liberal; the lower the score, the more conservative.

Differences by Unit

We looked first at single-unit measures of religion. Recall that these refer to 124 specific beliefs and behaviors like views of Scripture, views of salvation, and prayer. Table 9-1 shows that conservatives and liberals differ on relatively few of the units.[7] Of the many measures about the nature of God, for example, they differ on only three. There are no differences on religious behavior (e.g., prayer, church attendance), religious experience (e.g., born again), or religious centrality. When we compare specific beliefs and behaviors one by one, conservatives and liberals are more alike than different.

The differences that do occur suggest certain consistent tendencies worth noting. Political conservatives tend to make more references to self: "God has a plan for my life," definition of salvation as personal outcome, a self-restraint orientation, and God as a causal agent "in my life." Political liberals focus less on the self and more on the corporate: definition of salvation as social outcome, love as path to salvation, religion deals with corporate life, and an emphasis on social justice. The focus of conservatives tends more toward "me"; of liberals, more toward "we." Conservatives also emphasize three of the beliefs that form the nation-building religion discussed in chapter 6—"God has blessed America more than other nations," "God has chosen America to be a light to the world," and "God protects and preserves our social institutions and structures."

Differences by Scale

When we look at the thirteen religion scales described in chapter 8, we see the most dramatic ties between religion and political orientation. As table 9-2 shows,[8] liberals and conservatives differ on seven of the eight religious themes and on two of the three theological emphases.

The only religious theme not related to political orientation is Challenging religion; political liberals and conservatives are equally likely to expect behavioral change as a consequence of their religious beliefs. They do not differ on degree of Christian Orthodoxy nor on the two Importance scales.

Table 9-1. Religious Differences Between Political Conservatives and Political Liberals: Units

Category of Religious Belief†	Conservatives Are Higher on:	Liberals Are Higher on:
Religious beliefs: the nature of God	God is all-powerful* God is strict* God has a plan "for my life"*	
Religious beliefs: God's relationship to the world	God protects social institutions* God is a causal agent "in my life"*	
Religious beliefs: the means of apprehending God	—	—
Religious beliefs: salvation	Salvation is a personal outcome* A path to salvation is avoiding evil*	Religion addresses corporate life* Salvation is a social outcome** Love is a path to salvation**
Religious beliefs: eschatology	Life after death is certain*	
Religious beliefs: people and society	God has blessed America* God chose America*	
Religious beliefs: values and ethical principles	Self-restraint**	Social justice**
Religious behavior, experience, and centrality	—	—

*p<.01.
**p<.001.
†See Chapter 2.

How strongly related are these religious themes to political conservatism and liberalism? A statistic called the *correlation coefficient* shows the strength of the connection. Correlations range from −1.00 to +1.00. The higher the number (or the closer to

Table 9-2

Political Conservatives Are Likely to Score Higher on:	Political Liberals Are Likely to Score Higher on:	Political Conservatives and Liberals Do Not Differ on:
	Religious Themes	
Agentic	Communal	
Vertical	Horizontal	
Restricting	Releasing	
Comforting		Challenging
	Theological Emphases	
Evangelical	Symbolic God	Christian Orthodoxy
	Importance	
		Pro-Religion
		Pro-Church

+ 1.00 or − 1.00), the stronger the relationship. When a significant correlation occurs, it means there is a trend for two numbers (such as scores for Communal religion and political liberalism) to be related. If the correlation is positive, it means that people who score higher than others on Communal religion tend also to score higher on political liberalism. If the correlation is negative, it means that those higher on Communal religion tend also to be lower than others on political liberalism. And the larger the number, the stronger the association.

Table 9-3 shows the correlations between the nine discriminating scales listed above and the Americans for Democratic Action index of *political liberalism.*

That nine of the religion scales correlate this well with political orientation suggests that there are *major religious differences between liberals and conservatives.* The upper four in the list are particularly strong correlations, higher than those normally found when social scientists search for relationships between beliefs and behavior.

Differences by Type

The preceding chapter described six types of religion in Congress—Legalistic, Self-Concerned, Integrated, People-Con-

Table 9-3

Religion Scale	Correlation with Political Liberalism
Communal religion	.55***
Horizontal religion	.54***
Agentic religion	−.52***
Restricting religion	−.47***
Releasing religion	.33**
Vertical religion	−.32**
Evangelical	−.31**
Symbolic God	.28*
Comforting religion	−.23*

*p<.05.
**p<.01.
***p<.001.

cerned, Nontraditional, and Nominal. The types represent six different combinations of the religion scales. Since we have just seen that liberals and conservatives differ markedly on the scales, it seems likely that the six types would be located at different places on the political spectrum. Figure 9-1 shows this to be the case. The two types which emphasize Agentic, Vertical, Restricting themes—Legalistic religionists and Self-Concerned religionists—have the most politically conservative voting records of the six types. The two types which emphasize Communal, Horizontal, Releasing themes have the most politically liberal voting records. On the chart one can also see where the two types that balance the religious themes—Nominal religionists and Integrated religionists—fall on the political spectrum. Each takes a middle position on both the religious themes and politics, with Integrated tending toward the liberal political side and Nominal toward the conservative.

Why Are Religious Views and Political Orientations Linked to Each Other?

Why do we find such strong ties between nine of the religion scales and political orientation? It seems that there is a marked parallel between one's religious ideas and one's political ideas. To make this point clear we need first to undertake a step-by-

Figure 9-1. Six Religious Types and Political Orientation

| 100 | 75 | | 50 | | 25 | | 0 |

People-Concerned religionists (73)*
Nontraditional religionists (72)*
Integrated religionists (57)*
Nominal religionists (48)*
Self-Concerned religionists (27)*
Legalistic religionists (24)*

Liberal   Moderate   Conservative
Political   Political
Orientation   Orientation

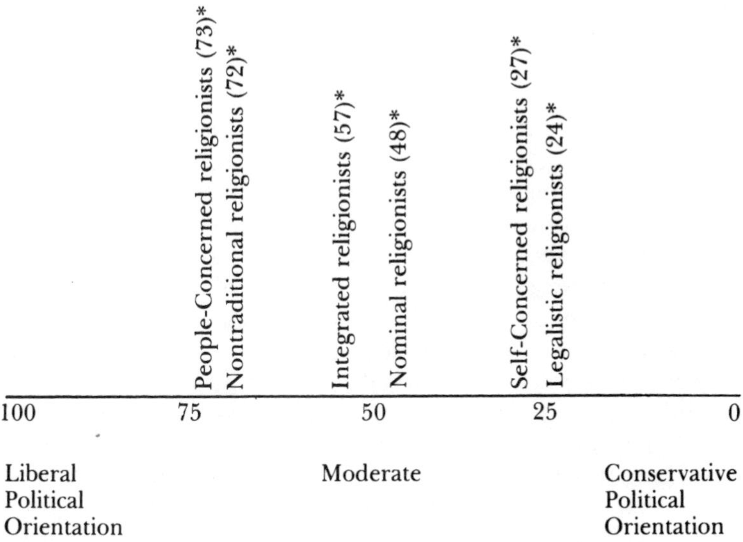

*Numbers indicate the group average on the 100-point measure of political liberalism.

step synthesis of what we have discovered about the religious perspectives of conservatives and liberals.

Connecting Threads

The connecting thread that runs through the political conservative's religion is the self. This religion encourages one to see the individual as God's major locus of involvement—God relates to individuals, saves individuals, makes plans for individuals. This is an emphatically Agentic religion, and it both reflects and reinforces the traditionally American idea that individuality is the cornerstone of human identity. The emphasis on self is also clear in the conservative's Vertical and Comforting orientations. Vertical religion stresses the individual's relationship to God, and Comforting religion implies that conservatives expect to receive support and reward from the religious life. Religion, for the conservative, tends to be for and about the individual. Religion helps one to function as an individual in the complex social world; God encourages this individualistic approach to life, gives one the strength and justification to adopt this life-agenda, and is expected to reward the individual for following it.

Up to this point the religion of the conservative sounds entirely self-serving and narcissistic. It would indeed be so were it not for the emphasis on self-restraint. The conservative's religion is Restricting: it provides abundant rules and obligations. When this factor is added to the Agentic/Comforting/Vertical components, we get an image of a religion which encourages individual freedom within limits. It is not a religion that gives permission for unconstrainted pursuit of individual ends. Rather, it promotes a more disciplined approach that puts boundaries on the pursuit of pleasure. This "liberty within limits" is reminiscent of the perspective common among the founders. It is not surprising, then, that conservatives are more likely than liberals to believe the basic tenets of the nation-building religion. Furthermore, it is not surprising that conservatives frequently call for a return to a traditional America.

Combining these elements into one unifying theme, we would submit that the religion of political conservatives is an *Individualism-Preserving religion*. It is a theology of individualism, where *individualism* means, as it does in philosophical circles, a pursuit of individuality balanced by an obligation for self-government.

The religion of political liberals has a much different cast. Its common thread is interdependence, its most pervasive focus on community, not individuality. Its message is: Think of yourself as part of a network of human relationships. Minimize the pursuit of individuality and seek rather to build bonds among people. Make self-expression and self-enhancement secondary to the needs of the human community. This message runs through the liberal's Communal religion and Horizontal religion. Communal religion reflects, in part, that God's purpose is to promote a corporate, relational posture to life in which people take care of each other. Salvation is not only something that happens to individuals, it happens to the earthly kingdom. It is a transformation of the social order. The liberal does not leave this work to God, but shares it. This is the meaning of Horizontal religion—a personally felt obligation to reach out to the world and transform it.

What sense do we make of the liberal's emphasis on Releasing religion? The statement central to this scale is, God liberates me, sets me free. Release from boundaries, from the way things are, is necessary to the change the political liberal sees as imperative if social justice is to be done. Society has usually not tended toward social justice to a degree satisfactory to liberals, so a frame of mind that seeks change is part of the liberal's total orientation to the world. The religion of liberals, which emphasizes Communal, Horizontal, and Releasing themes, is a *Community-Building religion*.

To this point, our argument suggests the scheme shown in figure 9-2.

Figure 9-2

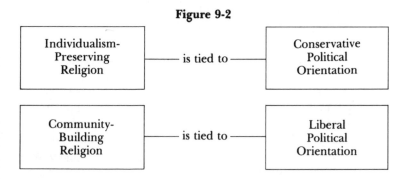

The discovery that two very different political orientations are associated with two very different religious orientations is an important one, and it invites some effort at explanation. To begin the explanation, we must be more precise in our characterization of conservative and liberal political orientations.

Conservative/Liberal Concepts of the Role of Government

Conservatives and liberals both seek human fulfillment and happiness. The major disagreement is on how best to pursue them. Political conservatives tend to adopt the premise that happiness best comes through allowing individuals maximum freedom to pursue their own economic and social rewards. The purpose of government is to ensure that as little as possible interferes with the pursuit of individual ends. Individuals are given the freedom to compete for wealth, property, and power —and government establishes the minimum number of rules and regulations necessary to keep opportunity accessible to everybody. In this competitive environment some persons cannot make it on their own. The conservative tends to see privately supported organizations (voluntary agencies like churches and charities) as the best means for aiding these persons, believing that the federal government runs welfare programs inefficiently and incompetently. The political conservative in Congress, then, is committed to promoting or preserving this doctrine of individualism.

The conservative's concept of the role of government is that it should:

- Interfere as little as possible in individual life.
- Encourage private ownership of the means of production; regulate private ownership as little as possible.
- Protect the free enterprise system, allowing individuals maximum opportunity to accumulate wealth.
- Promote a strong national defense so that the American system is not threatened by outside powers. The major enemies of conservative ideology and the capitalism it espouses are socialist and communist economic systems. Hence, national defense is necessary to protect our economic system from these forces.

Given the characterization, it is reasonable to hypothesize that conservative politics is really an Individualism-Preserving political orientation.

Liberal politicians believe problems arise as a result of "rugged individualism." They see large numbers of social victims—persons not able or not permitted to have equal access to opportunity and economic reward. They doubt the ability of the private sector to aid these social victims adequately. In an unconstrained competitive system a few accumulate wealth, many just scrape by, and some do not make it. Liberals say that government must broaden access to opportunity and reward. The values of the liberal, then, are centered less on competition and individualism and more on cooperation, sharing, and social leveling. These are Community-Building values.

The liberal concept of the role of government is that it should:

- Intervene in national life to protect civil liberties
- Assist social victims, or those who suffer from hardships, misfortune, or discrimination
- Regulate the free enterprise system to distribute economic rewards more equitably

The ties between religion and politics now become more obvious. They can be portrayed as in figure 9-3.

Figure 9-3

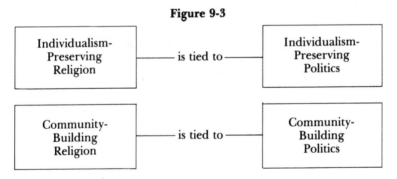

Seen this way, it is no wonder that religion and politics are connected. There is a clear symmetry between what one believes and values religiously and what one believes and values politically. In the field of psychology it is well known that persons seek a consistency among their ideas and ideals. The principle is called *cognitive consistency,* and the lack of consistency, or "dissonance," is uncomfortable. Accordingly, it would be troublesome to a person whose religion had a strong individualism theme to hold at the same time a view of politics which stressed community.

It is not surprising, then, that a member's religious views tie strongly to political views. If the theory is accurate, we should expect to find substantial correlations between religion and voting. And, indeed, we have demonstrated that Individualism-Preserving religion (Agentic, Comforting, Vertical, Restricting) and Community-Building religion (Communal, Horizontal, Releasing) appear at opposite ends of a general index of liberal political orientations. But do these different religious forms correlate equally well with how members cast votes on specific legislative and policy issues?

Religion and Voting on Specific Issues

Our theory can be used to generate a set of predictions about voting on specific issues. Individualism-Preserving politics minimizes government intervention in economic and social life, and advocates a strong national defense. This ideology, we reasoned, would translate into these four voting positions:

- Against government spending on social programs
- For private ownership of industry and business
- For resisting efforts by the federal government to compete with private enterprise
- For a strong military

If Individualism-Preserving religion and Individualism-Preserving politics are linked, we should expect to find Agentic, Vertical, Restricting, and Comforting religions correlating with each of these voting areas.

Community-Building politics, as noted earlier, seeks to distribute rights, economic rewards, and opportunity as broadly as possible, using the power of the federal government to bring about these ends. Community-Building politicians could be expected to take these voting positions:

- For the protection of civil liberties (such as voting rights, rights for homosexuals and other ostracized social groups, fair housing practices, and equal access to the judicial process)
- For programs and policies that help alleviate hunger and malnutrition
- For protecting reproductive freedom by providing econom-

ic assistance for abortions in cases of life endangerment, rape, or incest
- For extending economic assistance to developing nations

The religion–voting relationships we sought to test are summarized in figure 9-4.

Figure 9-4

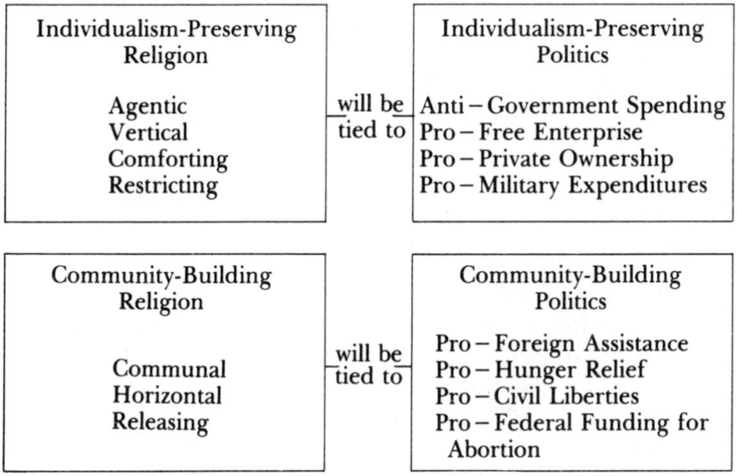

Individualism-Preserving Religion		Individualism-Preserving Politics
Agentic Vertical Comforting Restricting	will be tied to	Anti – Government Spending Pro – Free Enterprise Pro – Private Ownership Pro – Military Expenditures

Community-Building Religion		Community-Building Politics
Communal Horizontal Releasing	will be tied to	Pro – Foreign Assistance Pro – Hunger Relief Pro – Civil Liberties Pro – Federal Funding for Abortion

Each of the eighty members was given a voting score for each of the voting issues named in the right-hand boxes of figure 9-4. For each issue we noted a set of votes from the sources listed below, and calculated the percentage of the time that the member voted "correctly"—that is, in support of that particular issue. Each voting score falls somewhere between 0 percent and 100 percent. We then calculated the correlations between each of the thirteen religious scales and the voting scores. A brief description of the eight voting scales follows.

Anti–Government Spending: Based on votes cast on approximately two hundred bills involving federal spending. Prepared by the National Taxpayers Union on 1980 voting records.[9]

Pro–Free Enterprise: Based on free enterprise-related votes a member made in his or her entire congressional career, as tabulated by Americans for Constitutional Action in 1980.[10]

Pro–Private Ownership: Based on private ownership-related votes a Member made in his or her congressional careers, as reported by the Americans for Constitutional Action in 1980.[11]

Pro–Military Expenditures: Based on pro-military related votes cast by each member from 1970 to 1980, as compiled by the American Security Council.[12]

Pro–Foreign Assistance: Based on five votes cast in 1979 and 1980 on bills involving aid to developing nations in Central America, Africa, and Southeast Asia. Tabulated by the Friends Committee on National Legislation.[13]

Pro-Hunger Relief: Based on seven votes cast in 1979 on hunger-related issues as tabulated by *Bread for the World.*[14]

Pro–Federal Funding for Abortion: Based on five votes cast in 1979 on bills involving econmic assistance for abortions related to life-endangerment, rape, or incest, as compiled by *National Women's Political Caucus.*[15]

Pro–Civil Liberties: Based on six votes cast in 1980 on bills involving civil liberties, as compiled by the American Civil Liberties Union.[16]

The religion–voting relationships are presented in tables 9-4 and 9-5. A glance at the frequency and magnitude of the correlations between the religious themes and voting shows some important and substantial connections. On all the voting measures, at least six of the eight Religious themes show up as correlates. The Agentic, Vertical, and Restricting themes, which are the heart of Individualism-Preserving religion, are linked to each of the four Individualism-Preserving voting measures. And Comforting is linked to all except Pro–Private Ownership. The Communal, Horizontal, and Releasing themes, elements of Community-Building religion, are closely tied to the four Community-Building voting measures.

The major conclusion is this: members' religious beliefs and values are strongly connected to voting on specific issues, in ways that can be explained by our religion–politics theory.

Many of the correlations between the religious themes and

Table 9-4. Correlations of Thirteen Religion Scales with Voting on Four Conservative (Individualism-Preserving) Issues

	Anti–Government Spending	Pro–Military Expenditures	Pro–Free Enterprise	Pro–Private Ownership
Religious Themes	Agentic .53*** Vertical .27* Restricting .52*** Communal −.50*** Horizontal −.56*** Releasing −.32**	Agentic .59*** Vertical .28* Restricting .52*** Comforting .28* Communal −.53*** Horizontal −.57*** Releasing −.40***	Agentic .51*** Vertical .31** Restricting .43*** Comforting .29** Communal −.50*** Horizontal −.49*** Releasing −.30**	Agentic .35** Vertical .34** Restricting .29** Comforting .27* Communal −.38*** Horizontal −.31**
Theological Emphases	Evangelical .28* Symbolic God −.25*	Evangelical .29** Christian Orthodoxy .23* Symbolic God −.29**	Evangelical .29** Symbolic God −.32**	Evangelical .27* Symbolic God −.28*
Importance	No significant correlations	No significant correlations	No significant correlations	No significant correlations

*p<.05.
**p<.01.
***p<.001.

Table 9-5. Correlations of Thirteen Religion Scales with Voting on Four Liberal (Community-Building) Issues

	Pro – Foreign Aid	Pro – Hunger Relief	Pro – Government Protection of Civil Liberties	Pro – Federal Funding for Abortion
Religious Themes	Communal .59*** Horizontal .55*** Releasing .53* Agentic −.56*** Vertical −.37*** Restricting −.48*** Comforting −.31**	Communal .57*** Horizontal .56*** Releasing .34** Agentic −.54*** Vertical −.33** Restricting −.48*** Comforting −.24*	Communal .58*** Horizontal .56*** Releasing .43*** Agentic −.53*** Vertical −.31** Restricting −.51***	Communal .50*** Horizontal .54*** Releasing .31** Challenging .24* Agentic −.53*** Restricting −.49***
Theological Emphases	Evangelical −.34** Christian Orthodoxy −.27* Symbolic God −.35**	Evangelical −.30** Christian Orthodoxy −.23* Symbolic God .31**	Evangelical −.35** Christian Orthodoxy −.34** Symbolic God −.29**	Evangelical −.32** Christian Orthodoxy −.27* Symbolic God .26*
Importance	No significant correlations	No significant correlations	No significant correlations	No significant correlations

*p<.05.
**p<.01.
***p<.001.

voting are above .50. The Agentic and Communal themes are the most powerful, correlating at .50 or higher with all voting measures except Pro–Private Ownership. Social scientists experienced in tracking relationships between people's beliefs and their behavior would attest that these correlations represent particularly strong ties.

The theological-orientation scales are also connected to voting, though with noticeably less strength than the religious themes. Evangelical and Christian Orthodoxy orientations tend toward the same pattern as the Agentic, Vertical, Restricting, and Comforting scales: toward casting conservative votes, but only on some issues. Perception of God as Symbolic traces an opposite pattern, going with liberal voting and against conservative voting in a pattern duplicating the Communal, Horizontal, and Releasing scales.

That Evangelical and Symbolic theological orientations are associated with different voting styles is not surprising. An Evangelical orientation emphasizes a personal relationship with God—and so it has much in common with the individualism found in the Agentic, Vertical, Restricting, and Comforting themes. A Symbolic orientation deemphasizes this kind of individualism and is more compatible with the Community-Building themes—Communal, Horizontal, and Releasing.

The role of Christian Orthodoxy is more equivocal. Those who most affirm the basic tenets of the Christian faith are slightly more prone to take a conservative approach to *some* but *not all* voting issues. On three issues—government spending, free enterprise, and private ownership—members with high scores and members with low scores on Christian Orthodoxy vote similarly.

Conspicuous in their absence as correlates of voting are the Importance scales, Pro-Religion and Pro-Church. They are associated with none of the eight voting measures. This means that on these political issues members highly committed to the church do not vote any differently from those less committed to the church, and those who attach high importance to their religious world view do not vote differently from those who attach less importance. This is an important finding. It means that the amount or quantity of religion in a member's life is not tied to voting on these issues. It is when we are able to get deep inside a person's religious beliefs and values and discover how they operate dynamically in one's life—as we do with the eight religious themes—that we can see the substantial ways in which religion and voting are connected.

A word of caution is in order. It is important to remember that correlations are indicative of trends, not absolutes. So when we report that an Evangelical orientation is related in some cases to conservative voting (and then only in a rather modest way), we do not mean to report that all high-scoring Evangelicals are more conservative than low-scoring Evangelicals. If the correlation were around .90 or .95, then we could make that statement. But when the correlation is closer to .30, it only means that some, but not all, high-scoring evangelicals lean toward the conservative. In the next chapter we will be more precise about what percentage of Evangelicals are actually conservative voters. The same caution should be made about Christian Orthodoxy. The correlations of this scale with conservative voting are relatively modest and do not occur with all eight voting measures. When we look closely at those members who score toward the high end of Christian Orthodoxy and match them against the military-expenditures scale, we find 25 percent voting consistently against increased expenditures, 37 percent voting moderately (sometimes for and sometimes against), and 38 percent voting consistently for increased expenditures. With these numbers we can see that there is only a slight tendency for Orthodoxy to go with conservative voting.[17]

The Six Types and Voting

Because the eight religious themes relate so strongly to voting, it is probable that members who fall into the six types of religion found in Congress will cast votes similar to others of the same type and different from those of the other five types. Table 9-6 shows that this is indeed the case. The two types highest on the components that make up Individualism-Preserving religion—the Legalistic and Self-Concerned religionists—are the two most conservative types on all eight voting issues. Similarly, the two types highest on the elements involved in Community-Building religion—the People-Concerned and

Table 9-6. Six Religious Types and Voting

Voting Behavior	Legalistic Religionists		Self-Concerned Religionists		Integrated Religionists		People-Concerned Religionists		Nontraditional Religionists		Nominal Religionists	
	Average*	Rank†	Average	Rank	Average	Rank	Average	Rank	Average	Rank	Average	Rank
Pro–Civil Liberties	32	5	30	6	60	3	80	2	81	1	51	4
Pro–Foreign Aid	21	6	26	5	63	3	97	1	88	2	55	4
Pro–Hunger Relief	30	5	29	6	78	3	90	1	83	2	60	4
Pro–Funding for Abortion	23	6	28	5	71	3	87	1	86	2	44	4
Anti–Government Spending	47	6	45	5	25	3	23	2	22	1	34	4
Pro–Strong Military	84	6	78	5	44	3	19	1	26	2	58	4
Pro–Private Ownership	50	5	54	6	29	3	19	2	18	1	37	4
Pro–Free Enterprise	65	6	61	5	35	3	23	2	20	1	42	4

*Refers to the percentage of the time that members in a given type vote in accordance with Voting Behavior measures.
†Represents the rank order of the 6 religious types, with 1 designating the most liberal type on the issue and 6 the most conservative.

Nontraditional religionists—are always the most liberal voting types. The consistency with which different religious types vote is quite striking, as the columns labeled *rank* make dramatically clear. Note that on all eight voting issues:

- The People-Concerned religionists and Nontraditional religionists are the first and second most liberal
- The Legalistic religionists and Self-Concerned religionists are the fifth and sixth most liberal (which means they are first and second in conservative voting)
- The Integrated religionists always rank third and the Nominal religionists always rank fourth, following a middle course

The contrasts in average are also striking. Note, for example, that People-Concerned religionists vote for military expenditures only 19 percent of the time, whereas Legalistic religionists vote in favor of the military 84 percent of the time.

Perhaps the major point to be made about religion and voting is this: there is no one general statement that can capture the religion–voting connection. We cannot say that religious people vote differently than nonreligious people. We cannot say church attenders vote differently than nonattenders. We cannot say that members who are devout practitioners of religious ritual vote differently than the less-devout. Each of these is too general, too stereotyped, to capture what we now know. When talking about religion and voting in Congress, one rather has to preface his or her claims with "it depends." It depends on what kind of religion one is talking about. The paths between religion and politics are multiple. Some types of religion (those relatively more extreme in Individualism-Preserving components) go hand in hand with conservative voting; some kinds of religion (those relatively more extreme in Community-Building elements) go hand in hand with liberal voting; and some types (which are more moderate in location on the religious scale) go hand in hand with more moderate political behaviors. These multiple and varied connections between religion and voting have very little to do with religious affiliation. To know whether a member is a Catholic, a Protestant, a Jew, or even more specifically whether one is a Southern Baptist or an Episcopalian, tells us very little about voting. What matters is how religion is experienced, how it works and functions within one's life. These religious dynamics, occurring quite independently of church affiliation, are the "handles" that provide insight into how and why religion and voting are connected.

The Myths in Focus

> *Myth Number Three:* Political conservatives are more religious than political liberals.

The frequently voiced notion that political conservatives are more religious than political liberals has been fed from a number of sources. Detractors of institutionalized religion blame the church for turning people's attention away from crucial social problems and, accordingly, toward conservative thinking. The press focuses more attention on the religious right than on the religious left, further exacerbating the perception that religion and conservative politics are soulmates. Notable social theorists like Karl Marx and Herbert Marcuse have argued that religion is a conserving force, functioning to justify the status quo. As one social scientist has put it, "This intellectual tradition has produced a widespread and frequently uncritical tendency to conceive of religion as inerrantly conservative in such diverse areas as politics, economics, race relations, urban problems, and moral-ethical issues."[18] It is a belief widely held, even though there is research and theory available which argues to the contrary.[19] Nonetheless, the belief has such widespread currency in academic circles and among the press that it is not uncommon to hear it being generalized to settings like the United States Congress.

No matter how the claim is put—that conservatives are more religious than liberals, or that nonreligious members of Congress tend to be the most liberal—our findings indicate that it is not true. One key discovery was that Nominal religionists—those members least committed to religion—tend to be politically moderate rather than liberal, even tending a bit to the conservative side. Another was that liberals and conservatives do not differ on the two scales measuring Pro-Church and Pro-Religion. When we look closely at liberals and conservatives, we can conclude that they do not differ in the amount or quantity of religion. That is, they do not substantially differ in how often they go to church or read Scripture, or in their degree of commitment to religion or religious institutions. Liberals may be less orthodox in their belief, but their commitment is not less. The most accurate conclusion is this: *liberals and conservatives differ not in amount of religion, but in kind.* Overall, the conservative tends to adopt an Individualism-Preserving religion and the liberal tends toward Community-Building religion. The two groups of members march to different drummers, both politically and religiously.

> *Myth Number Four:* Religion bears little relationship to voting decisions.

Many observers of Congress, whether they are the press, political scientists, or the public, entertain the possibility that the religious views of members might inform voting on very specific moral issues, like abortion. There is, in fact, some evidence to support this view.[20] Beyond that, it is rare to hear a Congress-watcher consider the possibility that religion and voting may be intertwined. Textbooks and scholarly works on congressional voting, for example, pay religion scant attention.[21] It is simply not a topic of research or debate among most political scientists. In fact, some political commentators claim not only that there is not a religion–politics connection, but that there should not be, for such a tie would mean either that members are not objective or that the separation of church and state is being violated.

Voting in the U.S. Congress is in all probability a behavior that is determined by a combination of forces, all working together in some kind of complicated formula. We are not ready to claim that religious beliefs and values are the most crucial part of the formula. But we think our findings are strong enough to suggest that religious belief should join some of the more commonly recognized factors, like party affiliation and constituent pressure, as forces that bear on political behavior. On the basis of some additional analyses we discovered that, for many voting issues, knowing how members scored on three or four of the religious themes can tell us as much or more about how they will vote than knowing whether they are Republican or Democrat.[22]

Further Questions

There are still a number of unanswered questions about religion and voting. Our research ties religion to only eight specific voting issues. These eight represent only a small fraction of the issues confronting legislators. We cannot be sure that the conclusions we have made extend to all voting issues. We do not know whether the relationships will hold for topics like energy, ecology, health care, and agriculture. There indeed may be some issues on which voting bears no relationship to religious orientation. Those we selected for this study may be the very issues to which religious orientation is most powerfully linked.[23] These are important caveats. But we argue that in spite of these questions, the weight of the evidence is now more on the side of "religion is tied to congressional decision making" than on the side of "religion bears little relationship to voting."

We have been careful to avoid saying that religion determines voting. Our findings are based on statistical correlations between religion and voting, and a significant correlation between the two does not necessarily mean that one causes the other. All a correlation tells us is that two things (in this case religion and voting) go hand in hand.

Therefore, we cannot say for sure that religion *influences* voting, or *shapes* voting, or *guides* voting. We can say only that the two are related, linked, tied together.

This interpretation problem can be understood better by considering an analogy. Let's say that we found that smoking is correlated with anxiety. There are several possible causal sequences: the correlation might mean that smoking causes anxiety, or that anxiety causes smoking, or that some other factor—let's say occupational stress—causes one both to smoke and to be anxious. It would take additional research to establish which of these held the most truth.

And so it is with our findings. There are a number of interpretive possibilities, and it is premature to adopt any one as the truest. Figure 9-5 shows three possible interpretations (and there may be others).

If the first model is true, it would not be surprising to discover that the essential filter has to do with how the individualism–community issue is resolved. Whether one takes an "I" or a "we" approach to life could be shaped by one's religious heritage, and this, in turn, could lead to political perspectives that emphasize either Individualism-Preserving or Community-Building. If the "I" versus "we" orientation is as pivotal to life as we think it is, it is just as conceivable that this choice is made very early in life. Then, as one confronts an array of divergent religious and political ideas while growing up, one selectively holds onto those elements, both in religion and politics (as depicted in model *C*), that reinforce and solidify this basic posture toward life.

Figure 9-5

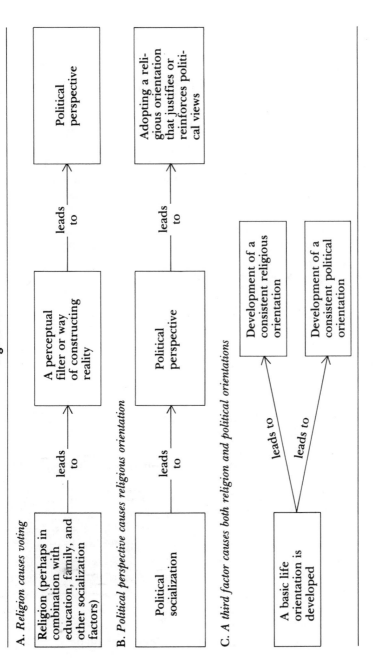

A. *Religion causes voting*

| Religion (perhaps in combination with education, family, and other socialization factors) | leads to | A perceptual filter or way of constructing reality | leads to | Political perspective |

B. *Political perspective causes religious orientation*

| Political socialization | leads to | Political perspective | leads to | Adopting a religious orientation that justifies or reinforces political views |

C. *A third factor causes both religion and political orientations*

A basic life orientation is developed — leads to → Development of a consistent religious orientation

A basic life orientation is developed — leads to → Development of a consistent political orientation

10. Profile of the New Christian Right in Congress

> *Myth Number Five:* Evangelical Christians in Congress are a united, conservative political force.
>
> *Myth Number Six:* Members of Congress who affirm basic Christian fundamentals adopt the politically conservative position of the New Christian Right; members who are atheists or secular humanists are politically liberal.

An important topic among those interested in either politics or religion, and of special concern among those who have always combined their interests in the two, is the emergence of the New Christian Right—its constituency, its methods, its platform, and its apparent power.

It is clear that something new has happened in political life; a whole new group has risen to national prominence, beginning with the national elections of 1980, and is making its goals and intentions clear. The general aim of the group can be summarized in the words of one of its most visible leaders, Jerry Falwell, as a desire "to turn America around in our lifetime . . . [to bring about] a moral America in which righteousness will exalt this nation. . . . The authority of Bible morality must once again be recognized as the legitimate guiding principle of our nation."[1]

The New Christian Right has become extremely controversial. Its rapid rise to national visibility has made it a focus of debate and discussion. A question of interest to the press, the mainline and liberal churches, and social scientists is, What religious world view fuels the New Christian Right's ultraconservative approach to politics? Two answers have been commonly presented. One view claims that evangelical Christianity spawns interest in ultraconservative politics. The other view, put forth by the leaders of the New Christian Right, is that commitment to the basic tenets of Christianity *compels* commitment to the political platform of the New Christian Right. In this chapter, we will demonstrate that both of these claims, when applied to the United States Congress, are seriously flawed.

What Is the New Christian Right?

Martin Marty, the noted American historian of religion, begins a recent article on the New Christian Right this way:

An encyclopedia of religion may soon have an entry like this: The New Christian Right is the generic term for a number of conservative and largely Protestant American political forces that surfaced in the elections of 1980. Best known of these was the Moral Majority, but Religious Roundtable and Christian Voice were among other sometimes overlapping, sometimes competing groups. Members were recruited by radio and television evangelists or through direct-mail techniques. Their clienteles were joined by congregants in fundamentalist local churches. Unlike their evangelistic predecessors, the new leaders advocated explicit political involvement. Theirs was a politics of nostalgia for an earlier "Christian America," and an opposition against "secular humanism" as the agent of moral decline in America. Among the chosen causes were opposition to abortion, disarmament, feminist and homosexual movements, and support of prayer and biblical teachings in Christian schools.[2]

The world view of the New Christian Right begins with the declaration that American society is on the brink of collapse, even extinction. The culprit is the moral decay that also finished off Rome as a world power. This decay, rampant throughout America, is responsible for all our national ills—inflation, military weakness, crime, unemployment. Because of this national immorality, it is said, we have gotten off the divine course—we have abandoned God's plan for America and are headed for trouble. Our political and economic decline makes us weak, and, as a consequence, the nation becomes ripe for a communist takeover. When that takeover happens, individual liberty will be gone, and with that will go our right to worship as we want. Then the nation will have gone to hell, quite literally, because we will no longer be allowed to hold or practice the faith that is the key to salvation.

How did we get into this mess? The real culprit, says the New Christian Right, is our national leadership. Rev. Jerry Falwell, president of the Moral Majority and its chief spokesperson, repeatedly points to Congress and other government officials as lacking the spiritual and moral principles necessary to keep the nation on its divine course. "As we look across our nation today we find a tremendous vacuum of godly men who are willing to be the kind of spiritual leaders who are necessary . . . to change a nation."[3] Our leaders, Falwell says, embody and encourage the sins of humanism, atheism, moral relativity, socialism, welfarism, and narcissism—and it is those values which threaten to destroy us. In sum, the theory says, we are a soft, weak, decadent nation, vulnerable to communist takeover, led by blind, godless, self-serving officials.

The solution to our problem has three parts. First, we must get God back on our side. James Robison, another key figure in the New Christian Right, says: "I believe the only real hope for the family and for America as a free nation is intervention by God himself to preserve the structures he has ordained."[4] Second, to merit that divine intervention, the nation must repent of its evil ways, and start living by God's principles: ". . . I do not believe God will step in until those who call themselves his people rise up, identify themselves, and take a firm stand for what they know to be right and godly."[5] The proof text for Falwell and Robison is Chronicles 7:14: "If my people, which are called by my name, shall humble themselves, and pray, and seek my face, and turn from their wicked ways; then will I hear from heaven and will forgive their sin, and will heal their land." Third, to bring about this national reformation we must have national leaders, particularly in the United States Congress, whose decisions will foster a national spiritual and moral reawakening.

The New Christian Right seems to have entered the political arena to make sure that we get the kinds of senators and representatives who will bring about this national cleansing. What exactly are the divine principles our elected leaders are supposed to favor? What does God want leaders to do to stop the slide into depravity and make way for God's providential hand to reenter our national life? The New Christian Right says that our nation and its leaders must:

- Stand against the Equal Rights Amendment
- Stand against the feminist revolution
- Stand against homosexuality
- Stand against secular humanism
- Stand against the social welfare system
- Stand against pornography
- Stand against abortion
- Stand against the eroding of male leadership in families
- Stand against the spread of Godless communism
- Stand against government spending
- Stand against busing for racial balance
- Stand against enacting penalties to segregated private schools
- Stand for restoration of prayer in public schools
- Stand for the free enterprise system
- Stand for increased military expenditure

This mandate has been divinely sanctioned, the theory continues. Each and every item in this list is said to have the full and unambiguous backing of Scripture. For example, Falwell says this about the Bible and capitalism:

The free enterprise system is clearly outlined in the Book of Proverbs in the Bible. Jesus Christ made it clear that the work ethic was part of his plan for man. Ownership of property is biblical. Competition in business is biblical. Ambitious and successful business management is clearly outlined as a part of God's plan for His people.[6]

In essence Falwell says that God has mandated political conservatism. It is right and moral because God wants it. A liberal political orientation is viewed as unbiblical, running counter to

God's will. Therefore, liberal voting is immoral, and Christians have a duty to purge Congress of its liberally inclined senators and representatives.[7]

The New Christian Right has begun a holy war in which the forces of evil are to be driven out by the forces of good. Everything is clearly defined. There are no uncertainties. We have the Bible, says the New Right, to back us up, and leaders appointed by God to lead the world to salvation. One of the Moral Majority's promotional brochures says that just as God sent forth Adam, Moses, John the Baptist, George Washington, and Abraham Lincoln in troubled times, he has now given the world Jerry Falwell.[8]

The groups most commonly associated with the New Christian Right are the Moral Majority, the Religious Roundtable, Christian Voice, and the National Christian Action Coalition.[9] Together they educate the public, raise money, enlist members, register voters, circulate newsletters, and mobilize clergy—all for the purpose of influencing social and political processes at the local, state, and national levels. The best-known operation occurred just before the 1980 national elections. Christian Voice developed a voting "report card" on each member of the Ninety-sixth Congress, assigning each senator and representative a score on a 100-point measure of Christian morality.[10] The score was the percentage of the time he or she voted in line with the issues enumerated earlier (e.g., opposing such issues as the Equal Rights Amendment, government aid for the medical cost of abortion, and school busing). Those who scored near 100 were viewed as moral; those who scored near 0 were considered less moral. Armed with this report card the New Christian Right created a "hit list" of members earmarked for defeat in the 1980 elections. Gary Jarmin, leader of Christian Voice, explained the process:

We have targeted about 35 members of Congress and the Senate who have scored low on our voting record and whom we think we can successfully retire from Congress in November. We're going to do up a little flyer showing exactly how the targeted Congressmen or Senators voted on these issues . . . , print up thousands of these and distribute these to Christians as they leave their churches on Sunday mornings.[11]

Jerry Falwell and the Moral Majority joined hands with Christian Voice and added six liberal senators to the hit list.[12]

It comes as no surprise that the targeted members were politically liberal, for the New Christian Right's platform is mostly a particular brand of conservatism. Many of the targeted members lost in the 1980 election. No one knows for certain how much credit to give to the New Christian Right's campaign against those members for the defeats. Many groups—among them the New Christian Right itself—are doing their best to estimate the impact.

In spite of the lack of an accurate estimate of its own power, however, one of the New Christian Right groups has announced its intention to develop a hit list of liberal senators for the 1982 election.[13]

We are witnesses to a fascinating chapter of American political history in which a new movement, employing a blend of old-time religion and far-right politics coordinated with Madison Avenue sophistication, is wielding considerable power. The criticism of the movement has, of course, been intense.[14] Many thousands of words have been written in an attempt to explain the rise of the New Christian Right. Our study affords us the opportunity to employ hard data to evaluate claims made about the religious underpinnings of the movement. We now turn to two of these claims.

Evangelical Christians and the New Christian Right

America has recently experienced, in addition to the rise of the New Christian Right, a national reawakening of the evangelical impulse. It has been widely assumed that these two movements are necessarily linked; many outside the evangelical camp believe that evangelicals are, almost without exception, politically conservative and supportive of the New Christian Right.

This stereotype was common even a decade ago, when the increase in evangelical sentiment first drew national attention. As one observer of the evangelical movement put it, those who are labeled *evangelical* are "rather automatically assumed also to be in or very near to the position of political right-wing extremists."[15] This assumption of a connection between evangelical

Christianity and conservatism has been fostered by recent stories in the national press. In 1980 the *New York Times* published a four-part series entitled "Ultraconservative Evangelicals: A Surging New Face in Politics." Stories in other leading print media have also treated the New Christian Right as an evangelical movement, thereby creating the assumption that evangelicals are "a vast pool into which the 'religious right' can ... dip."[16] A New York Times/CBS poll implied that the identity of U.S. evangelical Christians and the Moral Majority might well be the same, hazarding the guess that, if this were true, there might be as many as 67 million Moral Majority members or sympathizers.[17]

The stereotype also is applied to Congress. Mark Hatfield, the Oregon Sentator who is both an evangelical and a political liberal, has spoken often about the frequent assumption that evangelicals in Congress are a conservative political force. The press treats him as an interesting anomaly who violates the evangelical-equals-conservative rule. The title of a recent, widely distributed article, "Hatfield's an Evangelical, but a Liberal," reinforces the notion that to be both evangelical and politically liberal is unique.

To examine the stereotype of evangelicals in Congress, we first had to find a way to identify the evangelicals in our sample. Many people have tried to define the term *evangelical*.[18] After reviewing these varied definitions we decided that most could agree that an evangelical Christian has most or all of these characteristics:

1. A belief that Jesus is divine
2. A conviction that Jesus is one's personal savior
3. A discernible religious experience ("born again") in which Jesus entered one's life
4. A belief that Scripture is the Word of God
5. A conviction that God has a plan for one's life
6. A personal, on-going relationship with God
7. The habit of reading the Bible at least once a month

We decided to identify as evangelical any member in our sample for whom the first three characteristics were true and for whom a minimum of three of the remaining four were also true.[19] Twenty-two members (or 27.5 percent of our sample) met the criteria, a percentage comparable to what is found in the general public.[20]

We placed each of these twenty-two on two different political-orientation continua, as shown in figure 10-1. The first measure arranges our congressional evangelicals on the 100-point Americans for Democratic Action (ADA) measure of general political liberalism introduced in chapter 9. The second measure is the 100-point Christian Voice moral report card described earlier in this chapter. The two measures overlap somewhat, having some of the same votes in common. The Christian Voice index, however, was constructed with the New Christian Right platform in mind. On the ADA measure scores close to 0 imply political conservatism, whereas for the Christian Voice measure scores close to 100 imply political conservatism.

Evangelicals spread across the political spectrum. On both political-orientation measures about 40 percent of evangelicals tilt to the liberal side, and 60 percent are more at home on the conservative side. A fact as important as the spread is the polarization. The heaviest concentrations of evangelicals are at the extreme ends of the political continua. *There are very few evangelicals who take a moderate political position.*[21]

It is a serious overgeneralization to say that evangelical Christians in Congress are conservative. That statement is true for about 60 percent but not for the remaining 40 percent. Using the ADA measure, about one in four evangelicals (22 percent) are solidly liberal. Using the New Christian Right index, all 40 percent are solidly or extremely liberal. In chapter 9 we discovered that the evangelical scale correlated positively with conservative voting (though not nearly as strongly as did other religion scales). But sometimes we can rely too heavily on correlations. They are measures of trends, not absolutes. There is indeed a trend for more evangelicals to be conservative than liberal, and this accounts for the modest correlation. But we must also recognize the fact that there is a body of evangelical Christians who tend to vote with political liberals.

Figure 10-1. Political Orientation of Twenty-Two Evangelicals in Congress

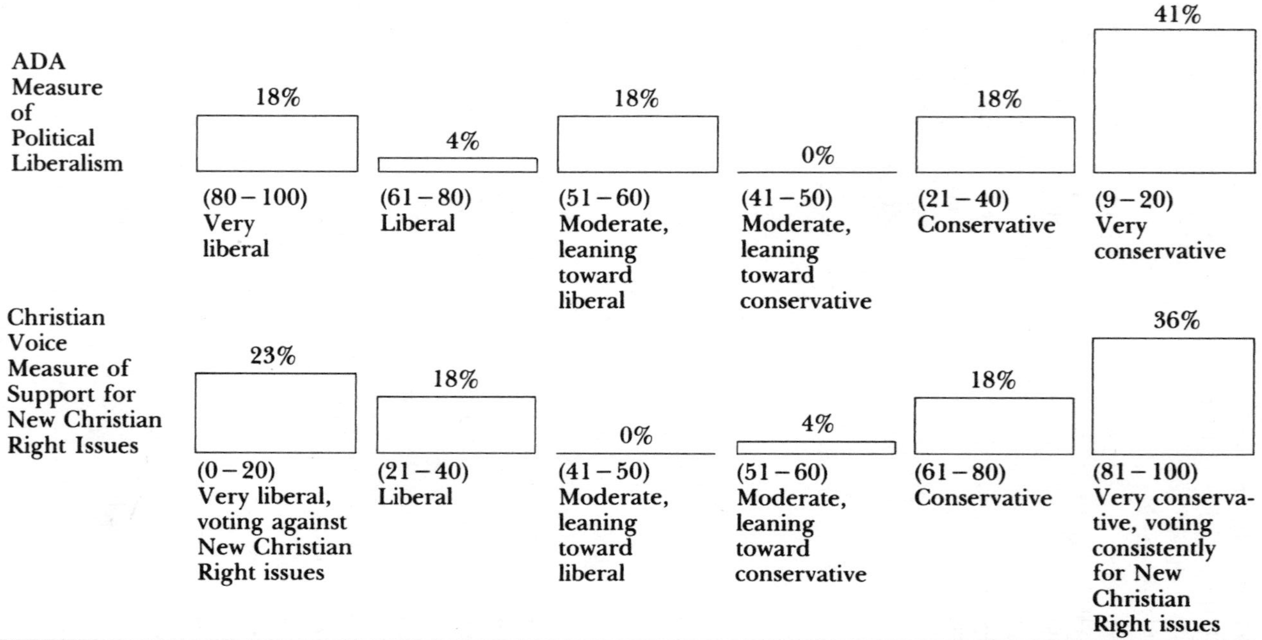

ADA Measure of Political Liberalism

18%	4%	18%	0%	18%	41%
(80–100) Very liberal	(61–80) Liberal	(51–60) Moderate, leaning toward liberal	(41–50) Moderate, leaning toward conservative	(21–40) Conservative	(9–20) Very conservative

Christian Voice Measure of Support for New Christian Right Issues

23%	18%	0%	4%	18%	36%
(0–20) Very liberal, voting against New Christian Right Issues	(21–40) Liberal	(41–50) Moderate, leaning toward liberal	(51–60) Moderate, leaning toward conservative	(61–80) Conservative	(81–100) Very conservative, voting consistently for New Christian Right issues

Note: Percentages refer to the percentages of twenty-two evangelicals who fall into each of the political-orientation categories.

Why are evangelical Christians who are united on a number of important religious issues so widely split when it comes to politics? We ran some special statistical analyses to compare the beliefs and values of evangelicals who lean to the left with those of evangelicals who lean to the right.[22] Not surprisingly, the differences are much like those we reported in chapter 9 as differentiating conservatives and liberals more generally. Of all the units and scales on which we can compare the two groups, three stand out as marking particularly strong differences.[23] These are:

1. *Salvation:* Conservative evangelicals view salvation only as individual immortality; liberal evangelicals think of salvation as both individual immortality and the transformation of society.
2. *Values:* Conservative evangelicals put major emphasis on self-restraint (minimizing vice, promoting virtue); liberal evangelicals, on social justice.
3. *Cause of social problems:* Liberal evangelicals are much more likely to see economic and political factors playing a causal role in problems such as poverty.

Whether these differences are entirely responsible for the political differences among evangelicals cannot be known for sure, but it does not take a very severe stretch of the imagination to entertain these as strong possibilities.

The Religious Beliefs of the New Christian Right

In the previous section we discovered that an evangelical religious orientation can lead either to a liberal orientation or to a conservative orientation like that adopted by the New Christian Right. If an evangelical orientation does not distinguish New Christian Right supporters from its detractors, what religious sentiments do?

Leaders of the New Christian Right boldly state what differentiates members of Congress who vote for New Right issues from those who do not. The claims, either directly stated or implicit, are these:

1. Those members who believe in basic Christian fundamentals—particularly that the Bible is the Word of God, Jesus is the divine Savior, and God is the ultimate authority—vote in line with the concerns of the New Christian Right.[24]

2. Those members who reject basic Christian fundamentals vote liberally.

3. Those members who value humankind vote with the New Christian Right, and those who selfishly value themselves vote liberally.[25]

These three propositions present the view that, if you are a Christian, there is only one right way to vote. The true Christian must find, and will find, that to vote conservatively is to be for God and to vote liberally is to be against God. These claims put things in neat boxes—politics is black or white. Either you are conservative and Christian, or a liberal, selfish, narcissistic atheist. The implication is that one cannot be a liberal and a Christian. Jerry Falwell quotes Senator Jesse Helms, a New Right proponent: "Atheism and socialism—or liberalism, which tends in the same direction—are inseparable entities."[26]

These claims were implicitly challenged in earlier chapters. In chapter 4 we noted that secular humanists are not common in Congress. Therefore the liberals in Congress could not all be secular humanists. And in chapter 9 we concluded that political conservatives and liberals do not differ on the basic tenets of the Christian faith. But that conclusion was based on dividing members into conservative and liberal groups based on the Americans for Democratic Action (ADA) index of political orientation. The New Christian Right uses the Christian Voice measure of political orientation to pinpoint conservatives and liberals. While the two measures overlap somewhat in the votes they examine, they are not identical. And so to more fairly test the claims of the New Christian Right, we used the Christian Voice index to divide members into those who support the views of the New Christian Right (and are therefore conservative by its own definition) and those who oppose those views (and are therefore liberal by its definition), and then compared their religious views. We placed the twenty-two members who scored below 15 on the 100-point scale in the *Opposers* group, and the twenty-one members who scored at 85 or above in the *Supporters* group.

We find that none of the New Christian Right claims are accurate. Supporters and Opposers are equally committed to God, Scripture as the Word of God, and Jesus as Savior. Liberals who vote for school busing, government spending, abortion rights in cases of incest and rape, social welfare programs, and cutting military spending are just as likely as the supporters of the New Christian Right's agenda to adopt the basic tenets of Christianity. Furthermore, liberals and far-right voters are equally likely to experience God in a close and personal way, read Scripture, and attend worship services.

Table 10-1

Supporters of New Christian Right Positions		Opposers of New Christian Right Positions
Percentile		*Percentile*
	Individualism-Preserving Religion	
86	Agentic	14
70	Restricting	19
60	Comforting	32
66	Vertical	30
	Community-Building Religion	
26	Communal	79
25	Horizontal	79
34	Releasing	70

Nonetheless, the Supporters and the Opposers do have important religious differences. But the differences are not in the areas pointed out by the New Christian Right. We should not be surprised to discover that New Right Supporters and Opposers differ in ways we found true of conservatives and liberals in general. The New Right Supporters place relatively high emphasis on the four elements that comprise Individualism-Preserving religion—Agentic, Vertical, Comforting, and

Restricting—and deemphasize the Community-Building Horizontal, Releasing, and Communal scales. We can see these differences by looking at the percentile scores for the Opposer and Supporter groups. (See table 10-1.) The percentile scores tell us how much a group is above or below the midpoint of the fiftieth percentile. Although the groups differ noticeably on all seven religious themes, the most graphic difference is on the Agentic theme.

We get a clearer picture by looking at how the Opposers and Supporters fall into the six religious types. (See figure 10-2.) The New Christian Right Supporters in Congress have no representative in the Integrated and People-Concerned categories. Most of its support comes from the Legalist and the Self-Concerned categories. In sum, the religion of the New Christian Right appears to place minimal emphasis on reaching out to people, but instead is maximally devoted to promoting and governing the interests and welfare of the self. Opposers of the New Christian Right positions are spread more across the six types. Most Opposers belong to the Integrated, People-Concerned, and Nontraditional types for whom commitment to translating one's beliefs into helping create a more just social system (Horizontal) is primary and for whom Community-Building is a general religious disposition.

It is clear that the claim that "those members who value humankind vote with the New Christian Right, and those who value themselves vote liberally" is not true. The evidence seems to point in the other direction.

One other vote about New Right Supporters: In addition to placing high importance on Individualism-Preserving religion, they also have a stronger belief than more liberal voters in the elements of the nation-building religion described in chapter 6. Nearly all affirm that "God protects and preserves our social structures," "God has chosen America to be a light to the world," and "God has blessed America more than other nations." As we noted earlier, these nation-building beliefs fit well conceptually with Individualism-Preserving religion, for they reflect a commitment to the primacy of individual liberty.

Figure 10-2. Religious Types and the New Christian Right

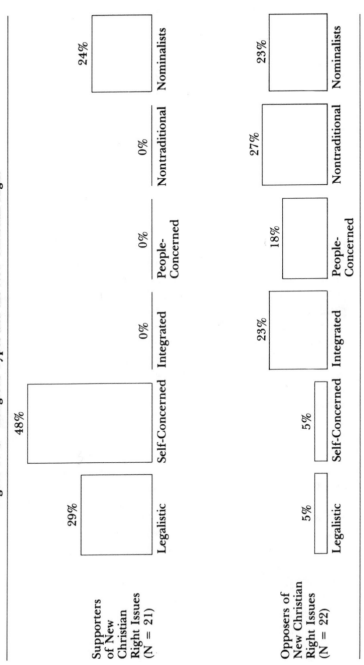

Supporters of New Christian Right Issues (N = 21)

29%	48%	0%	0%	0%	24%
Legalistic	Self-Concerned	Integrated	People-Concerned	Nontraditional	Nominalists

Opposers of New Christian Right Issues (N = 22)

5%	5%	23%	18%	27%	23%
Legalistic	Self-Concerned	Integrated	People-Concerned	Nontraditional	Nominalists

The Myths in Focus

> *Myth Number Five:* Evangelical Christians in Congress are a united, conservative political force.
>
> *Myth Number Six:* Members of Congress who affirm basic Christian fundamentals adopt the politically conservative position of the New Christian Right; members who are atheists or secular humanists are politically liberal.

Contrary to the claims of the New Christian Right's leaders, one cannot judge sincerity, depth, or centrality of religious convictions by looking at the voting behavior of members of Congress. We find that political liberals who vote for things like reproductive freedom, civil liberties, and social welfare are just as likely to affirm Christian principles as those who vote against abortion, against social welfare, and for military spending. The ties between religious belief and political orientation are much more complex than the New Christian Right would have us believe. Sincerely religious people can be political conservatives, moderates, or liberals.

The leaders of the New Christian Right are so far off the target in their claims that Christianity leads only to conservative politics and that political liberals are "godless humanists" that one wonders why the claims are even made. Some social analysts see it as the old political game of tarring and feathering the political opposition with labels the public abhors, hoping the labels will stick. This game is reminiscent of the McCarthy era, when, as now, in the short run it did not make any difference whether the labels were true. What mattered was getting people to believe them.

Another possible explanation for the erroneous claims made by the New Christian Right is a narrow view of religious ethics. One noted scholar sums it up this way:

Many outsiders, offended by the New Christian Right's exclusivism and its arrogant-sounding identification of its claims with the Word of God, hope that in the course of time its members will find more elements of that Word of God in their cherished Bible. The Bible *does* have something to say against pornography and obscenity and *may* have something, however ambiguous, to say about the rights of homosexuals and fetuses. The Scriptures clearly do have much to say about the misuse of wealth, the alliance between the powerful against the poor, the distribution of resources, stewardship of the earth and the cause of peace.[27]

It would be a different matter if the New Christian Right, recognizing a broader range of ethical obligations, said to the liberals of the country: "Let's each take on separate battles. We'll focus attention on the personal vices of individuals. You liberals focus on the social conditions that cause some of the corporate vices of the world, like poverty and social inequities. We'll both be doing needed work." This kind of approach would recognize the legitimacy of different religious values. It would also make it illegitimate to assume that liberals *en masse* are atheists or to develop hit-list campaigns to get liberals out of office.

It is chiefly the fact that the movement says, "The values we prize are the only legitimate ones," that causes problems to arise. It is this claim of having a monopoly on truth that repels many who share some of the aims of the New Right but cannot adopt the movement's claim of exclusive truth and its attacks on liberals. It is an exclusive-truth claim that makes villains of anyone who thinks differently. It violates the American tradition of religious pluralism. It stops dialogue and debate, and polarizes people. In that kind of political milieu decisions become increasingly irrational—both for the attackers and the attacked—and the whole political system suffers. Senator Barry Goldwater, a political conservative, recently said of the New Right: "The uncompromising position of these groups is a divisive element that could tear apart the very spirit of our representative system. . . ."[28]

Our analysis of the New Christian Right has been premised mainly on the views of Rev. Jerry Falwell, founder and leader of the Moral Majority, the largest and most visible of the so-called New Christian Right groups. We do not know if his views prevail among all those who consider themselves part of this political movement. There may be a diversity of views among leaders and followers that has not yet come to light.

There are signs that Falwell and others connected with the New Christian Right have softened their rhetoric since 1980. Some have been more willing to compromise and to listen to alternative points of view in recent days. How the various segments of the New Christian Right conduct themselves in the 1982 and 1984 national elections will tell us much about whether their leaders have indeed begun to muffle their claims of exclusive truth. Until that happens they will continue to be isolated, by their own design, from the remainder of the religious world—a world with which they might otherwise sometimes join in mutual respect and toward common purposes.

11. New Perspectives on Religion in Congress

MANY OF the most important interpretations of our findings have already been stated in earlier chapters, along with the data that support them. However, there still remain a few useful things unsaid, a few overall conclusions to draw.

This book tells a story that has about it some of the aura of a shotgun marriage. It tells the tale of two elements of life that have not generally been acknowledged to be in relationship, but that have in fact been linked for a long time. A combination of scientific curiosity and circumstance forced the rumor of the union into the spotlight. Now it seems that since the fact of the linkage has been demonstrated, we might as well acknowledge it in the open, rob it of its subterranean quality, and let it take its place among other recognized relationships in the sphere of knowledge.

There will, of course, continue to be some in both families—those in the political world and those in the religious world—who object to the marriage because of some long-standing, dearly held views about the way things are or ought to be. Nevertheless, while religion and politics may not live happily and in perfect serenity ever after, there will at least not be the strain on anyone of trying to pretend that the relationship does not exist.

Religion, Politics, and Our Discomforts

Our discovery that religion and voting are tied in strong, predictable, and explainable ways in the U.S. Congress will come to some as unwelcome news. Although we have taken care to acknowledge that what we have uncovered are only connections, and that we do not yet understand the relationship in terms of cause and effect, nevertheless even the possibility of such a relationship may cause discomfort. We envision four possible sources of that discomfort.

1. *It troubles me that you take something from the spiritual realm— religion—and connect it with the competitive, sometimes manipulative, generally shady world of politics.* There are those in the religious world who do not like the implication that religion has a demonstrable connection with something so this-worldly, pragmatic, and tinged with the image of the smoke-filled room as politics. They would prefer that religion keep clear of the world of commerce, political influence, and other such mundane and unspiritual matters. The belief they articulate is a variety of a first-century heresy called *Gnosticism*. The belief, perhaps oversimply expressed, is that all things spiritual—God, a person's soul, a person's prayer and worship life—are good. All things material—eating, jogging, making love, buying and selling things, voting—are evil, or, if not evil, then certainly second-class and to be separated as much as possible from spiritual things. Seen from this point of view, the ultimate goal of life is to become completely oriented to the spiritual and entirely detached from the material.

This belief has persisted throughout the ages, always in conflict with another view which accords more closely with the message most groups within the Judeo-Christian tradition have historically proclaimed. An important function of religion, in this second view, is to influence and improve *all* of life. In carrying out this purpose, religious people consider themselves properly engaged in working with and among the mundane and unsavory, working to make life more humane, just, and satisfying for everyone. In this view, religion is not just permissible in the political arena; it belongs there.

2. *The constitutional division of church and state prohibits mixing of religion and politics.* One common misreading of the intent of the Constitution is to assume that the division of church and state extends to make a division of religion and politics mandatory as well. But the Constitution speaks only of the former. Probably as a shield against the kind of religious intolerance

that flourished in prerevolutionary Europe, the nation's founders were explicit about religious freedom. The First Amendment to the Constitution states that "Congress shall make no law respecting an establishment of religion, or prohibiting the free exercise thereof. . ." The government, in other words, shall neither promote nor inhibit particular forms of religion. Not only was the promotion of religion actively practiced by the state in Europe, but in some of the colonies as well, where taxes supported certain churches and followers of certain other religious traditions were disenfranchised. It was that kind of official connection that the Constitution was designed to prohibit.

There is a persistent confusion between separation of church and state, which is the law of the land, and separation of politics and religion, which is impossible. Religion, when taken seriously, becomes so interwoven with the identity and world view of the person who holds it that it cannot be separated from political choices or any other of the choices the person makes.

The right of individuals to practice their chosen religion was granted by the Constitution. Does the Constitution then give individuals the right to bring their religious beliefs to bear on political issues? To try to persuade voters or the Congress to take a particular position for acknowledged religion-related reasons? Absolutely. The right has been upheld a number of times by the Supreme Court.

3. *I want my elected representatives to be objective and value-free, open to hearing the arguments of all sides.* As long as we persist in electing human beings to serve in Congress, complete objectivity and value-free decisions will be impossible. All of us bring our heredity, our past experiences, and our various filters—including the religious filter—to our work. A member can make an attempt at hearing all sides, and many do. But after all sides are heard, it is the member who decides. It is too much to expect that members will have no personal leanings, tendencies, or biases that enter into the voting decision.

4. *Does your study mean that members vote their ideals rather than the will of the constituents?* In spite of our heavy accent on the tie of religion to voting, we make no claim that it is the only influence or even the strongest influence. It is likely one of many influences, another of those being the voice of the constituent.

The formula by which members make voting decisions is far from clear, and religion might enter the formula in various ways. It may affect the way in which members hear constituents, and thereby indirectly influence voting. It may affect the way in which members choose colleagues as trusted friends, and thereby narrow the range of their influence. It may operate differently in different instances, influencing some votes quite strongly and directly and others much less so.

Religion and the Myths Disproved

What can we make of the religion–politics connection? What can we expect to be different as a result of our knowledge about it? To begin with, it rids us of some misleading notions that have led down some divisive and unproductive paths in the past.

The evidence strongly suggests that the U.S. Congress, far from being a hotbed of secular humanism, agnosticism, and atheism, is instead made up of a preponderance of people to whom religion is important, most of whom belong to a church or synagogue, and most of whom engage in both the public and the private practice of their faith.

We know that members of Congress are not less religious than the rest of the American public; if anything, in some ways of defining religiousness, they are more religious than the American public.

We know that being religiously committed does not automatically brand one as a political conservative, but that a goodly number of the committed tend to be liberal in voting pattern, and some among the committed are the most liberal of any in Congress. And when we look at a particular brand of conservatism—that represented by the New Christian Right—we still find conservatives and liberals holding many beliefs in common.

[We know that it can be shown with some certainty that a member's type of religious belief is predictably connected with a substantial range of voting issues.]

We know that evangelical Christians in Congress are not a united voting bloc. On the contrary, the members who score highest on our evangelical measures tend to divide and cluster at opposite ends of the political liberal–political conservative continuum. On the voting measures we used, few evangelicals are politically lukewarm or moderate.

It is hard to let go of some of our favorite myths. However, the shattering of a myth now and then can do wonders for one's outlook on life. It lets new light in. Now that some of the mist has cleared, there may be assumptions to reexamine and a private collection of villains and heroes who now require new labels.

With the myths shattered the public experiences some new uncertainties in place of the assurances that the old stereotypes provided. There was a time when the public believed one could expect the evangelical candidate to be conservative. One could expect the liberal candidate to be less subject to influence by religious principles. One could expect the candidate backed by the New Christian Right to be more religious than the other candidate. The trouble with those expectations was that there was a potential for later disappointment when the candidate, once elected, turned out not to support the "right" causes.

Voting, like politics, is an inexact science. A voter can never be certain what characteristics, biases, tendencies, and convictions come along with the person for whom the ballot is cast. The choice is difficult. Candidates for a given office often sound rather alike. If one understands politics and religion about equally well, or knows the political world better than the religious world, those politically tuned perceptions are probably a good index to the voting choices that must be made.

However, if you are a person who wants to vote intelligently and whose ear is much better attuned to religious issues than to political issues, it may be possible to use that religiously astute ear as you listen to candidates. Does the message mark him or her as more of a Legalist or more of a People-Concerned type? Does the candidate sound more like a Nontraditional or a Self-Concerned? In the religious realm, does the candidate seem to want to urge the morality that he/she espouses onto all of society? Does the candidate talk more about the need for control and for adherence to the laws of God, or about encouraging the development of people's God-given potential? These are matters cental to the religious identities that connect to some voting issues. If our evidence is correct, what you hear in the religious realm may turn up in related voting patterns, once the candidate is elected.

Religion—A Less Global View

Many people, in thinking about religion, tend to think in large, sometimes loosely defined categories, making some general assumptions that, if they are led to look at them carefully, they would agree the evidence does not entirely support.

One of our first convictions is that religion for most is more than window-dressing, more than something tacked onto life. One clergyman described the tacked-on religion as being treated in many conversations as if it were a kind of green glop that can be splashed onto things to make them seem religious. Live as you like, but splash on a little green glop by sitting through a worship service now and then. Conduct a business meeting in which all members employ against each other their sharpest manipulative skills in an effort to get their own way, but splash on the green glop of religiosity by opening or closing the meeting with prayer. We found some evidence that some in Congress may adhere to the green-glop theory, but they are a minority. Some, too sophisticated to think of religion in that way, still think in general categories that show up in sentences that begin "Catholics tend to ..." or "Jews usually are ..." or "Religious people are ..." There is something dynamic about religious belief, when taken seriously, that causes it to be integrated into the person's total perception of life, into his or her motives and ways of dealing with people and decisions. This integration process produces great variety among religious people, so that, like snowflakes, no two of them are exactly alike.

Not only does religion exert power in life, but there seems to be evidence that its development is interactive—the person interacting with the religious messages he or she receives to develop a particular religious type. Obviously there is some process at work that causes members of the same denomination, hearing the same kinds of messages delivered from the religious institution, to turn out to have very different sets of belief. Individuals may be quite active participants in the development of their own religious world view and posture, finding and internalizing the religious themes and messages that best accord with who they are.

If we assume that most persons can be located in a religious type, a number of significant questions emerge. What accounts for one's location in a religious type? Why have some become Self-Concerned religionists while others are People-Concerned? Do people move, across their life span, from one type to another? Once a person is established as a Self-Concerned religionist, is no further change likely? Could there be a sequential movement from one type to another throughout life, as there is evidence for in stages of moral reasoning? And if people move, by what process does it occur?

Religion and Behavior

This study is, at the surface level, about the ties that exist between religion and political decision making. We think the ties were unearthed because we endeavored to find a way to get inside a person's religion—beyond the surface evidences of religiousness—to mine a deeper and more productive level of information. We presented interview questions specifically designed to explore eight ways of defining how religion works in people's lives (Agentic, Communal, Vertical, Horizontal, Releasing, Restricting, Comforting, and Challenging). Armed with these themes we found substantial connections between them and political behavior.

The question of how religion relates to voting in Congress is only the preamble to a much larger question: How does religion relate to all behavior? Voting is only a small and easily accessible part of all the behaviors possible for Congress, and the range of behaviors available for study in the general population is even broader.

Psychology is a discipline devoted to understanding human behavior. It is appalling to discover how little psychologists know about religion. Religion is a major element in life for many people, and yet this element is rarely looked at or studied by psychologists. In textbook after textbook, whether on clinical psychology, developmental psychology, or social psychology, religion is rarely mentioned.

Some of the hesitance to study religion may come from not knowing how to measure religion or how to identify what one is looking for. Our study provides a starting place for other studies of the link between religious belief and behavior.

It seems reasonable to assume that some human tendencies represent an individualistic posture: achievement, competition, assertiveness, and aggression. Might it not be fruitful to investigate how the components of the Individualism-Preserving religion are linked to some of these? Likewise, some human tendencies are more communal: altruism, empathy, cooperation, friendship formation, and affiliation. An understanding of these behaviors could be expanded by looking at how they connect with Community-Building religion themes.

Search Institute has been investigating the relationship of religion to human behavior for twenty-three years. If our experience is to be trusted, it tells us that psychologists will find—if they look—that religion is a powerful predictor of the behaviors they seek to understand.

Religious Types in Later Congresses

How representative are our discoveries, and how durable? The facts and interpretations presented in this book are based on interviews with eighty members of the Ninety-sixth Congress, whose term ran from 1978 to 1980. Do our myth-shattering discoveries hold true for that entire body of 535 members? We think the eighty are a good representation of the entire Ninety-sixth Congress, as shown in chapter 2, although we do not want to overstate that claim. Having achieved contact with a sample that closely matches the entire Congress as to Senate-House membership, political party, region, religious affiliation, sex, age, education, and voting record, everything we know about research would say that our sample accurately represents the whole. We cannot know whether there is something about the thirty-two of the originally drawn sample whom we were not able to reach that makes them very different from our sample. On paper they do not seem to be different. In the absence of absolute certainty we can state that we believe (but do not know) that their inclusion in the sample would not have significantly altered the information we have presented.

Evidence, observed from a distance, is that the Ninety-seventh Congress, serving from 1980 to 1982, is made up of members with religious commitments at least as strong as those held by the Ninety-sixth. The turnover of members between the two congressional terms was too small to make a dramatic change in the overall portrait of religion in Congress. If the efforts of the New Christian Right were as successful as it hopes, the presence of religious conviction should be stronger in the Ninety-seventh than in the Ninety-sixth.

In coming years, as Congresses come and go, what change might we see in the religious makeup and behavior of Congress? Certain things will not change. We would not expect the substantial connections between type of religion and voting to be altered. Nor would we expect the identity of the six religious types—Legalist, Self-Concerned, Integrated, People-Concerned, Nontraditional, and Nominal—to change. We might see, however, a change in the proportion of members that falls into each of the six types.

Religion in the Wider World

Although much of what we have presented has meaning in the Congress, our discoveries also say some important things about religion. We think it likely that the religious themes and religious types described in this study would find their counterparts almost anywhere in the general population. We believe that this book has implications in the wider world.

Although the six religious types were discovered in analysis of interviews with members of Congress, the religious scales and types afford new descriptive labels and definitions that can help us understand varieties of religious belief and expression throughout the Judeo-Christian world, and perhaps beyond. It seems likely that other populations, people in other walks of life—scientists, homemakers, clergy, academics, the general public—could easily find a home in one of the six types. The proportions of the six types might vary, but all could fairly easily be found and identified.

If this generalization of the types to the population at large is possible, we then have new categories in which to diagnose and reexamine our own religious tendencies. We have occasion to evaluate the nature of the filter with which we hear and incorporate certain messages ("... some seed fell into good soil") and fail to hear others ("... and some seed fell on rocky ground"). We have opportunity to observe whether our religious type compels our own behavior only when patently religious matters are at issue, or whether we carry that tendency into other areas of life. If we are Legalists religiously, are we also Legalists at home and at our place of work?

A corollary discovery may be that there is considerable potential for dialogue across different religious groups. A widespread warming of relationships between individuals and small groups from different denominations has occurred over the past twenty years or so. This warming has enabled them to work meaningfully in joint historical and liturgical studies, social-action projects, and a variety of other enterprises. This phenomenon is probably further evidence of the truth that religious types spread across the denominations. When representatives of Catholic, Lutheran, Presbyterian, and Jewish faiths have found themselves able to work well together, it may have been because they are of similar religious types and thus are able to work from shared assumptions, in spite of the division of churchly allegiance and divergent ritual. With that recognition they have been able to band together to work on common ground, from common assumptions.

Religious Tension—Friend or Foe?

One of the cherished hopes we may one day have to relinquish is the warmly good-hearted assumption that, since a given group of people is composed entirely of a single religious tradition, it ought to be able to agree. Reason, experience, and the evidence of our research combine to discourage that hope. Religious people receive the message of their faith in such markedly different ways that people with equal religious conviction and commitment (insofar as these can be measured) often express themselves in sharply opposing kinds of behavior.

For example, people vary in their willingness to introduce into ordinary daily conversation references to the joy of their relationship with an ever-present God. Certain believers, particularly those who carry the Companion God concept (of chapter

3), are in the habit of delivering testimony about their relationship with God, sharing it publicly with whoever will listen. This emphasis on religious conversation grates on some—particularly on those who hold an Attentive Parent concept of God, whose view of God includes more of mystery, and majesty, and "otherness." These people see too frequent mention of God's action in life as a trivialization of the power of an awesome being and are both embarrassed and made resentful by the implication that, because they do not talk frequently and publicly about God, they are not appropriately committed.

During the congressional interviews, some members expressed their discomfort with their evangelizing, testimony-giving colleagues. Said one, "If they want to wear religion on their sleeves, that's fine. But let's not make that a mark of the true believer." The tension between believers in Congress on this point is a reflection of the same tension all across America, in large and small churches, in Bible study groups, in places of work and play, between those who talk easily about their religion and those who don't.

Nor is this the only tension that exists. Chapter 8 described four pairs of religious themes that not only underlie the six religious types but also form the structure and the dividing point for disagreement among religious people both in Congress and across the religious world.

There is a constant tension between the Vertical and the Horizontal themes, between those who see religion as a private relationship between them and God and those who view religion as a force which binds them to others in community. This tension shows itself even in such a home-grown way as in a battle over where parish announcements ought to be placed in the worship service. The Vertical message is that the announcements ought to be eliminated altogether from services of worship and communicated at some other time, since the worship service is primarily for individuals to commune with God. Horizontals see the announcements as an important expression of the life of the religious community, integral to corporate worship.

The Comfort–Challenge tension becomes particularly visible at budget-setting time in churches. One faction will recommend that the remainder of the budget be pared down in order to release funds to serve needs in the surrounding community. Others will quickly rise to point out the distressing condition of the roof and the constantly increasing costs of operating the building and the congregational program.

One place where the Releasing–Restricting tension is visible is in the messages a church delivers to believers about childrearing. The Restricting message ("Train up a child in the way he should go . . .") emphasizes parent-set rules and speaks of parental responsibility for the shaping and control of the child—such control being not only in the child's best interests but innately right. The Releasing message ("Let the children come, . . . for of such is the kingdom of Heaven") will emphasize ways to nurture and foster a child's God-given potential by offering a climate of freedom to express feelings and opinions. In most churches both elements will be present, but one or the other will be emphasized.

The tension between people who are of the People-Concerned type and those who are of the Legalist or Self-Concerned type becomes visible when groups try to set the first priorities of the church. The People-Concerned will express the belief that the paramount task of the church is to be a servant in the world. This will be countered by those who believe that the needs of the congregation are paramount. The servants-in-the-world believe that the major task is outreach. They want to employ the power of the church in ministering to those whom society seems to have forgotten. The Legalists and Self-Concerned are likely to acknowledge the need to serve the outside world, but they will also say that it is inappropriate—even potentially disastrous—to concentrate too great a proportion of attention, leadership skill, and funds outside the church. "Sometime later," they will usually say, recognizing the legitimacy of the outreach message, "but not now. We aren't ready / can't afford it / need to get our own house in order first."

In the midst of these tensions it is possible that the greatest discomfort will be suffered by the Integrated religionists. In our congressional sample the Integrated type scored high enough on both sides of the tension—relatively high on both Vertical and Horizontal, reasonably high on both Comfort and

Challenge—that they can see the logic and truth in the arguments advanced by both sides. Although they may feel more pain in such arguments, they are also in the best position to be able to build some blessed but temporary bridges of understanding between opposing factions.

One of the major messages carried in the mass of data summarized in this book is that religion affects people differently, even those who take it equally seriously, and therefore *the tensions that exist in our varying points of view are not likely to go away.* We have not all the same gifts—nor the same perceptions, nor the same agendas, nor the same ways of living our religion.

But that is not altogether bad news. Though tension and struggle are painful, good often comes of them. The religious establishment as well as the rest of society needs a variety of pressures to keep it on course. Some must sound the note of caution, some give the challenge to action, some point the way to change, some point to the value of stability and tradition. Part of our American belief in the value of pluralism causes us to see that the church, the Congress—indeed, all of society—is best served when all sides continue to speak their convictions. The tensions are essential to the health of the organism, provided of course that there also exist enough mutual respect, trust, and shared area of agreement so that the tension does not tear it apart.

It is here that members of the New Christian Right go astray, and with them others—individual people, whole denominations, cults—who believe that theirs is the only way. As was illustrated in chapter 8, all of the positions expressed in the religious themes can be supported with Scripture. The New Christian Right and other "only way" people find themselves on shaky grounds and lose potential friends when they declare that the *only* message Scripture has to deliver is the one they claim as support for their position.

Given the admission of this continuing tension, what is the value of pointing out the tension? By looking straight at those things that divide us, and acknowledging those divisions, we can sometimes move away from the scene of battle and look again at what unites us, at where the agreements and concurrences are. A visible difference is usually more manageable than an invisible and unacknowledged one. The "management" may be only a matter of avoiding the disputed territory whenever circumstances make it possible. When avoidance is impossible, we may shorten the conflict by recognizing and acknowledging the other's already known and stated position.

It is interesting to consider what would happen if sermons and other messages conveyed by religious institutions were delivered individually, like medical prescriptions, designed specifically for the greater health of the person for whom they are prescribed. For the one who needs more exercise, the doctor can prescribe it. For the one who is running herself into a state of fatigue, the doctor can advise a slowdown.

Instead, it is the practice of the church to deliver all messages to everyone. At one point it offers a word of challenge, at another a word of comfort, at another a message of the release that comes through the understanding of truth, and at still another the value of standards and self-discipline. At one point the charge is sounded to go out and revolutionize the world; at the next the message comes that we should be still and know that God is God, and that one serves in stillness and waiting.

It seems apparent that listeners hear most clearly the parts that reinforce their already existing belief systems, and hear only faintly the parts that oppose. One wonders whether it would be better if we were sorted into categories by some cosmic diagnostic process and issued only the messages that we most need to hear. Perhaps the urging of the church toward individual reading of Scripture and individual prayer is intended, in part, to expose us to the cosmic diagnostic process. The messages each of us most need to hear may be the very ones that are hardest for us to absorb. Perhaps we can hear them best when we are concentrating, and quiet, and alone.

When it comes to the question of religion, of the ways in which we understand God and ourselves and what that relationship means, when it comes to the question of our commitment to our religious beliefs and the ways in which we live them out, there is very little difference between the members of Congress and the rest of us.

We elect them from among us. Though we often view them as the enemy—the *they* in Washington who vote our taxes and delimit our freedoms—in the immortalized words of Pogo: "We have met the enemy, and they is us." The same varieties of pressures, longings, and dreams motivate us all. The same personal hurts and physical limitations and human suffering assail us. August as the congressional office seems to most of us, and awed as one nearly always is by the power it wields, before God the office holder and the home-town voter are much the same.

What we have learned about Congress, therefore, we have probably also to some extent learned about ourselves. Perhaps as we reflect on what we see through this window on one of the hitherto unexplored corners of life, we will find some new understanding, some increased respect, some common ground for hope.

Appendix A.
Questions of the
Congressional Interview

1. [Member is handed a card listing the five statements below.] The first question I'd like to ask you is whether you believe in God or some ultimate Religious Reality. Please choose which statement on this sheet most applies to you.
   A. I don't believe in God or an ultimate Religious Reality (some power, being, force, or energy that holds things together and influences the world's destiny).
   B. I don't think it is possible for me to know whether God or an ultimate Religious Reality exists.
   C. I am uncertain but lean toward not believing in an ultimate Religious Reality.
   D. I am uncertain but lean toward believing.
   E. I definitely believe that God or an ultimate Religious Reality exists.
2. Which of these six pictures best symbolizes God's relationship to the world?
   A. God and the world are one.

   B. The world is part of God, but God is greater and larger than the world.

C. Human beings are part of God.

D. God sets the world in motion but does not play an active role in the world.

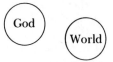

E. God transcends the world, entering the world infrequently.

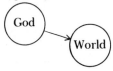

F. God transcends the world but is actively involved in the world.

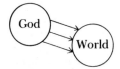

3. Is God a personal being who has feelings, consciousness, and a will? Or is God something else?

4. When you think of God, what three or four qualities come to mind?

5. [Member is shown list below.] I am interested in hearing how true each of these eighteen phrases about God is for you. As I read each one in the list, indicate how true it is for you by using a number from one (not at all true) to five (extremely true). God is . . .

A. Faithful and dependable
B. Unapproachable
C. Forgiving
D. Mysterious
E. More present in relationships than in individual lives
F. Distant
G. Permissive
H. A creative force in history
I. Aware of everything I think and do
J. Close

K. Vindictive
L. My constant companion
M. Strict
N. Clearly knowable
O. In my life more as a symbol or an idea than as a real presence I can feel
P. All-powerful
Q. Both awesome and fascinating
R. Judging

6. Did our sprint through these eighteen descriptions of God give you ample opportunity to describe what God is to you? Or are there ideas about God you would like to add or highlight?

7. [Member is handed a card listing the five statements below.] Which of these five statements is truest for you?
   A. God is the *strongest* influence in my life.
   B. God is a *very strong* influence in my life.
   C. God has a *moderate* influence in my life.
   D. God has a *small* influence in my life.
   E. God has *no* influence in my life.
8. If you wanted to help someone who did not believe in God to find God, where would you tell him to look? In Scripture? In nature? Inside oneself? Or where?

[For questions 9–24.] How true for you are each of these statements? I'm looking for your off-the-top-of-the-head response. Feel free to comment.

9. God works to protect and preserve our social institutions and structures.
10. In their lifetime, God sometimes punishes those who are evil and rewards those who are good.
11. God did not play a role in the writing of Scripture.
12. Society cannot survive without religion.
13. God has blessed America more than other nations.
14. God has chosen America to be a light to the world.
15. There is one religious tradition that is truer than all other traditions.
16. Everything in Scripture is absolutely true and factual.
17. I come to know God better through the church.
18. Wealth is a sign of God's favor.
19. The church often inhibits the development of mature religious faith.
20. God has a plan for my life.
21. God accepts me as I am.
22. God is always just and fair.
23. God liberates me, sets me free.
24. God, like persons, is constantly evolving and changing.
25. Who was Jesus?
26. What does Jesus mean to you?
27. [Member is handed a paper showing the diagram below.]

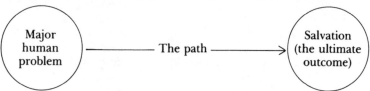

Religion commonly speaks to three issues:
—a major human problem
—an ultimate outcome, often called salvation
—a path to this ultimate outcome
What is the human problem your religion deals with?

28. What is the ultimate outcome? What is salvation?
29. What percentage of people do you think attain salvation?
30. What is the path to salvation? How does one get there?
31. Is there life after death? What is it like?
32. In life after death, is individuality lost or preserved?
33. What difference, if any, does your religious faith make in your life? How, if at all, are you different because of what you believe?
34. In what way, if any, do your religious beliefs and values get in the way as you serve in Congress?
35. To what degree do your religious beliefs and values guide or influence your voting decisions?
36. [Member is handed a sheet listing the eight responses below.] Generally speaking, how much do each of the following have to do with determining what happens in people's lives?
    A. God
    B. Satan, or some evil force
    C. The exercise of free will
    D. The social system—its economic and political arrangements
    E. One's values and motives
    F. The kind of environment one grew up in
    G. One's abilities and skills
    H. One's inherited traits and capacities
37. [Member is handed a sheet listing the six responses below.] Which of the following images of human nature are true for you?
    A. Predominantly evil, sinful
    B. Selfish, competitive
    C. Predominantly good
    D. Loving, cooperative
    E. Perfectible, given the right social conditions
    F. Not perfectible; there are no social conditions that can overcome human evil
38. There are two common positions on the best way to approach social problems (e.g., crime, violence, pollution). One approach says that the best way to address these problems is by changing the hearts of individuals. The other calls for transforming institutions and structures. Which one is closest to your position?
39. Which of the following two statements comes closest to your view?
    A. American society is very close to meeting God's expectations for what a society should be.

    B. American society is a long way from fulfilling God's expectations.

40. If you had the power to change one thing in American society, what would it be?

41. What do your religious beliefs and convictions tell you about how you should lead your life? What should be your priorities in life? What should you seek to be or do? Try to give me as many words or phrases as possible.

42. What religious group or church body do you identify with?

43. Are you currently a member of a church or synagogue?

44. How often do you attend worship services?

45. What leadership roles, if any, have you taken in the church or synagogue?

46. Have you ever had college or graduate work in religion or theology?

47. How often, if at all, do you pray?

48. How often, if at all, do you read Scripture?

49. Which, if any, of these religious experiences have you had?

    A. The experience of having God speaking to me

    B. The experience of feeling God's presence

    C. The experience of feeling one with God

    D. The experience of feeling united with the universe

    E. A born-again experience in which Jesus entered my life

    F. The experience of speaking in tongues

    G. The experience of specific answer to prayer

50. On the graph, please draw a line that best represents how important religion has been to you in your life.

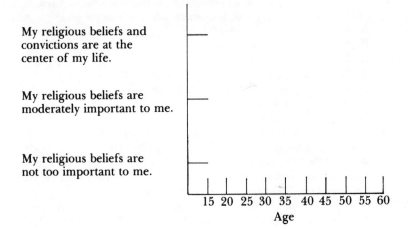

My religious beliefs and convictions are at the center of my life.

My religious beliefs are moderately important to me.

My religious beliefs are not too important to me.

15 20 25 30 35 40 45 50 55 60

Age

Appendix B.
Profiles of Six Types of Religion
on Eight Religion Scales

THE MARKED points on the charts that follow represent the average score on the eight religion scales for the members of Congress surveyed who comprise the six religious types. On each chart only the locations of the scores of that one type are labeled, though all other scores are represented by unlabeled points.

The upper four are Agentic-complex scales, so designated because the Agentic scale is sufficiently powerful (both conceptually and statistically) to draw the other three with it into a coherent set. This set of scales represents the concerns of the individual—individual goals, individual relationship with God, rules to protect individual rights, and the comfort and solace of the individual.

The lower four are the Communal-complex scales, all cohering around the Communal scale. This set represents concerns for the group, for justice, for a religion that frees, and a faith-inspired impetus to action.

From study of the charts one can discover the range represented for each scale; for example, the lowest-scoring group on the Agentic scale received a score of 40, and the highest-scoring group received a score of 57 (numbers are marked at the bottom of each chart). One can also see visually presented some of the characteristics that distinguish one group from another.

Legalistic religionists strongly emphasize the four themes of the Agentic complex. On the lower four themes even the highest score is lower than the lowest of the Agentic-complex set. The highest score of all for Legalists is the Restricting theme of rules, boundaries, limits, and guidance. That devotion to clear limits, together with their strong tendency toward emphasizing all of the other Agentic-complex scales, is what most strongly distinguishes Legalists from others.

The Self-Concerned religionists show a pattern of scores similar to that of the Legalists, with the Agentic-complex scores falling generally higher than any of the Communal-complex scores, with the notable exception of the Challenge scale, whose scores rises almost as high as the highest of the upper four scales. Like the Legalists the Self-Concerned tend toward strong Agentic-complex scores, but unlike the Legalists they are strongly challenged to action by their faith.

Integrated religionists' scores reverse the tendency of the first two types. All of their Communal-complex scores are higher than their Agentic-complex scores, but they tend to achieve a balance between the two sets. They show only one extremely high score (Releasing) and no extremely low scores.

The People-Concerned religionists' scores carry the tendency of the Integrated religionists a step farther, emphasizing even more strongly the tendency toward high scores on the Communal-complex set, demonstrating a marked gap between the two sets. They show extremely high Horizontal concerns and rank at the top of both the Communal and Challenge scales. Of their Agentic-complex scores, the Vertical—relationship-with-God—score is highest, almost matching the level of the Releasing score.

Nontraditional religionists show the most extreme contrasts of any group between the Agentic-complex and the Communal-complex scores. An appreciable distance separates their highest score on the upper set and their lowest on the lower set. They show the lowest scores on every element of the Agentic-complex set. They are not oriented strongly to their own agenda, they have little prayer life, their religious beliefs do not emphasize rules and limits, and they seem to value religion less for its Comfort than any other group. Their high Communal and Horizontal scores combine to identify this group as very much concerned with cooperative effort and justice for all.

Nominal religionists' scores trace a middle-of-the-road line down the eight scales, revealing no marked preference for either the Agentic complex or the Communal complex. Their only extreme score—lowest on Challenge—assures us that, whatever else motivates them, it is not their religious belief.

Legalistic Religionists

Agentic Complex

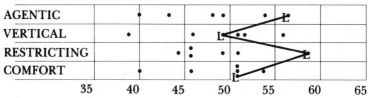

Communal Complex

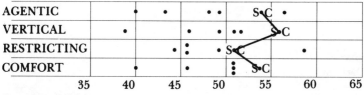

Self-Concerned Religionists

Agentic Complex

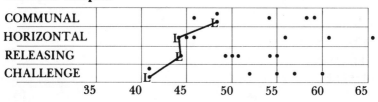

Communal Complex

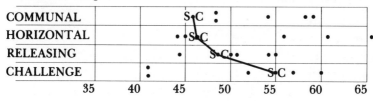

Integrated Religionists

Agentic Complex

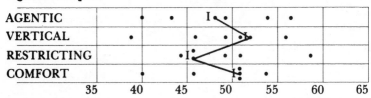

Communal Complex

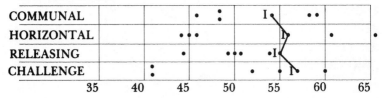

People-Concerned Religionists

Agentic Complex

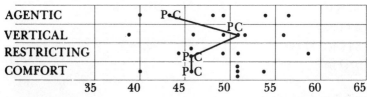

Communal Complex

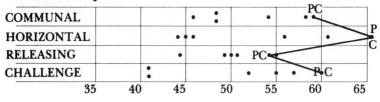

Nontraditional Religionists

Agentic Complex

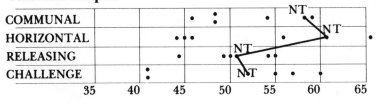

Communal Complex

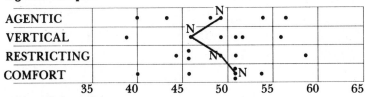

Nominal Religionists

Agentic Complex

Communal Complex

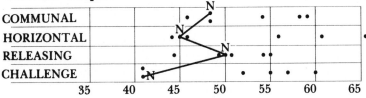

Notes

Chapter 1

1. See, for example, the collection of essays in John B. Anderson, ed., *Congress and Conscience* (Philadelphia: J. B. Lippincott, 1970).
2. For an analysis of how religious affiliation relates to voting on abortion, see Maris A. Vinovskis, "The Politics of Abortion in the House of Representatives in 1976," *Michigan Law Review* 77 (August 1979): 1790–1827. Of related interest are two studies by James T. Richardson and Sandie Wightman Fox which investigated the ties between abortion and religious affiliation in state legislatures: "Religious Affiliation as a Predictor of Voting Behavior on Abortion Reform Legislation," *Journal for the Scientific Study of Religion* 11 (December 1972): 347–59; and "Religion and Voting on Abortion Reform: A Follow-up Study," *Journal for the Scientific Study of Religion* 14 (June 1975): 159–64. Albert J. Menendez is one of the few scholars who has explored how religious affiliation relates to other voting issues in the U.S. Congress. See his *Religion at the Polls* (Philadelphia: Westminister Press, 1977).
3. Merton P. Strommen, ed., *Research on Religious Development: A Comprehensive Handbook* (New York: Hawthorne Books, 1971).
4. We also attempted several empirical investigations of social desirability. For example, for those members facing election in 1980, we correlated the religion variables with the percentage vote each received in the 1978 national election. We reasoned that those who "squeaked by" in 1978 might be particularly motivated to "look good" in 1980. No notable relationships were found between expressed belief or reported behavior (e.g., church attendance, frequency of prayer, certainty of God's existence) and margin of victory in 1978. In later chapters we discuss the strong correlations between religion and voting. If many members had given distorted accounts of their beliefs and values, it is unlikely that these powerful and systematic relationships would have emerged.

Chapter 2

1. For an analysis of unconventional religion in America, see Robert S. Ellwood, Jr., *Alternative Altars: Unconventional and Eastern Spirituality in America* (Chicago: University of Chicago Press, 1979).
2. This definition of religion was particularly informed by the work of David Little and Sumner B. Twiss, *Comparative Religious Ethics: A New Method* (San Francisco: Harper & Row, 1978). The definition is substantive rather than functional. That is, religion is defined in terms of its content or substance rather than in terms of what it does. For more on this distinction, see Peter Berger, "Some Second Thoughts on Substantive Versus Functional Defini-

tions of Religion," *Journal for the Scientific Study of Religion* 13 (June 1974): 125–33.

3. The seven categories have been broken down further into approximately 150 subcategories. This taxonomy of religious beliefs is available from the authors.

4. The random sample was stratified on three variables: party affiliation (Republican, Democrat, Independent); region (East, West, Midwest, South); and religious affiliation (liberal Protestant, mainline Protestant, conservative Protestant, Catholic, Jewish, unknown). See notes to table 2-2 for information on how religious traditions were classified.

5. Biographical information on each member of the Ninety-sixth Congress was taken from two sources: Michael Barone, Grant Ujifusa, and Douglas Mathews, *The Almanac of American Politics, 1980* (New York: E. P. Dutton, 1979); and the *1979 Congressional Quarterly Almanac*, pp. 33–42.

6. Seventy of the eighty participating members were tape-recorded. Four members were interviewed face-to-face but chose not to be tape-recorded. The remaining six members completed a written version of the interview.

7. In May 1981 a team of four coded the interviews. Nine interviews were coded by all four, forty-two by two coders working independently, and twenty-nine by individual coders. Coder agreement across all items was better than 80 percent. On most items coder agreement was 90 percent or higher. On minor disagreements (e.g., one-point difference between coders on five- or six-point items), the average rating between coders was used. On all major disagreements, including any disagreement on placements in categories, coder teams discussed the item until agreement was reached. Coders used both the tape-recording and a typed transcript of the interview to make their judgments. Coders were blind to members' party affiliation, name, and political orientation.

Chapter 3

1. For examples of research on God-images and their relationship to other domains, see Merton P. Strommen, Milo L. Brekke, Ralph C. Underwager, and Arthur L. Johnson, *A Study of Generations* (Minneapolis: Augsburg Publishing House, 1972); Thomas Piazza and Charles Y. Glock, "Images of God and Their Social Meaning," in *The Religious Dimension: New Directions in Quantitative Research,* ed. Robert Wuthnow (New York: Academic Press, 1979); and Peter L. Benson and Bernard Spilka, "God-Images as a Function of Self-Esteem and Locus of Control," *Journal for the Scientific Study of Religion* 12 (September 1973): 297–310.

2. Two books by Robert S. Ellwood, Jr., discuss the location of this alternative religious view in American society: *Religious and Spiritual Groups in Modern America* (Englewood Cliffs, N.J.: Prentice-Hall, 1973); and *Alternative Altars: Unconventional and Eastern Spirituality in America* (Chicago: University of Chicago Press, 1979).

3. Monism is usually seen as a subcategory of pantheism. See George F. Thomas, *Philosophy and Religious Belief* (New York: Charles Scribner's Sons, 1970), for an elaboration of this point.

4. Robert Flint, *Anti-Theistic Theories* (Edinburgh: William Blackwood & Sons, 1889), p. 336.

5. For a discussion of panentheism see Charles Hartshorne, *Man's Vision of God and the Logic of Theism* (Hamden, Conn.: Anchor Books, 1964).

6. Max Weber, *The Protestant Ethic and the Spirit of Capitalism* (New York: Charles Scribner's Sons, 1958).

7. See J. Alan Winter, "Quantitative Studies of the Applicability of the Weber Thesis to Post World War II U.S.A.: A Call for Redirected Efforts," *Review of Religious Research* 16 (Fall 1974): 47–57.

8. Rodney Stark and Charles Y. Glock, *American Piety: The Nature of Religious Commitment* (Berkeley and Los Angeles: University of California Press, 1968).

9. Quoted in *Time*, September 29, 1980, p. 85.

10. Thomas, *Philosophy and Religious Belief*, p. 49.

11. G. Van der Leeuw, *Religion in Essence and Manifestation*, 2 vols. (New York: Harper Torchbook, 1963), 2: 681–82.

12. Alfred Braunthal, *Salvation and the Perfect Society* (Amherst: University of Massachusetts Press, 1979), p. 33.

13. For a discussion of this point see Melford E. Spiro, *Buddhism and Society* (New York: Harper & Row, 1970).

14. Strommen et al., *Study of Generations.*

15. See John Hicks, *Death and Eternal Life* (New York: Harper & Row, 1976), for a review of life-after-death images.

16. For an excellent review of several different systems of values and how these relate to other aspects of religion, see Little and Twiss, *Comparative Religious Ethics.*

17. Tim LaHaye, *The Battle for the Mind* (Old Tappan, N.J.: Fleming H. Revell, 1980), p. 17.

Chapter 4

1. These figures differ from those on church attendance because they incorporate other forms of church activity in addition to participation in worship services.

2. This technique was suggested by Sheridan P. McCabe, University of Notre Dame.

3. The correlation between these two measures is .58, $p < .001$.

4. For each of these dimensions coders assigned the interviewer a number on a seven-point continuum. On approximately 90 percent of the ratings coders either assigned identical numbers or numbers that departed from each other by one.

5. This analysis was based on seventy-seven members. For three members, missing data made accurate classification unlikely.

6. This quote is from an untitled paper on the definition of religion prepared by James Dittes for this project.

7. S. Robert Lichter and Stanley Rothman, "Media and Business Elites," *Public Opinion* (October/November 1981): p. 43.

Chapter 5

1. Jerry Falwell, *Listen America!* (New York: Doubleday, Bantam Books, 1981), p. 17.

2. Ibid., p. 14.

3. This study is available from Connecticut Mutual Life Insurance Co., 140 Garden St., Hartford, CT 06115.

4. Connecticut Mutual Life Report, p. 201.

5. Princeton Religious Research Center, *Religion in America, 1979–1980* (Princeton, N.J.: 1980).

6. Because of these problems and related statistical issues like confidence intervals, we decided to focus our attention mainly on differences larger than 10 percent.

7. Strommen et al., *Study of Generations.*

8. *Emerging Trends,* May 1980, p. 3.

9. See p. 197 in *Sex, Profanity, and Violence: An Opinion Survey about Seventeen Television Programs,* a report prepared for NBC in June 1981.

10. Kenneth S. Kantzer, "The Charismatics among Us," *Christianity Today,* February 22, 1980, p. 25.

11. *Emerging Trends,* January 1979, p. 2.

12. Peter L. Benson, "Religion on Capitol Hill," *Psychology Today,* December 1981, pp. 46–57.

13. For an analysis of how the media influence public opinion on political issues, see W. Lance Bennett, *Public Opinion in American Politics* (New York: Harcourt Brace Jovanovich, 1980).

Chapter 6

1. John Devotion, *The Duty and Interest of a People to Sanctify the Lord of Hosts* (Hartford, Conn.: Eben Watson, 1777), p. 39, as quoted in Mark A. Noll, *Christians in the American Revolution* (Washington, D.C.: Christian University Press, 1977), p. 77.

2. Noll, *Christians in the American Revolution,* p. 30.

3. Winthrop S. Hudson, *Religion in America,* 2d ed. (New York: Charles Scribner's Sons, 1973), p. 60.

4. Ibid., p. 67.

5. Ibid., p. 76.

6. Norman Cousins, *In God We Trust: The Religious Beliefs and Ideas of the American Founding Fathers* (New York: Harper & Row, 1969), p. 8.

7. Ibid., pp. 8–9.

8. Hudson, *Religion in America,* p. 92.

9. G. Adolf Hoch, *Religion of the American Enlightenment* (New York: Thomas Y. Crowell, 1968).

10. For a discussion of civil religion see Robert N. Bellah, "Civil Religion in America," *Daedalus,* Winter 1967, pp. 1–21.

11. Sydney E. Ahlstrom, *A Religious History of the American People,* 2 vols. (Garden City, N.Y.: Doubleday, Image Books, 1975), vol. 1.

12. Catherine L. Albanese, *Sons of the Fathers: The Civil Religion of the American Revolution* (Philadelphia: Temple University Press, 1976), p. 113.

13. See ibid., p. 114, for this general idea.

14. Adrienne Koch and William Peden, eds. *The Life and Selected Writings of Thomas Jefferson* (New York: Random House, 1944), pp. 706–7.

15. Herbert Richardson, "Civil Religion in Theological Perspective," in *American Civil Religion,* ed. Russell E. Richey and Donald G. Jones (New York: Harper & Row, 1974), p. 164.

16. Robert N. Bellah, "American Civil Religion in the 1970's," in *American Civil Religion,* p. 255.

17. Koch and Peden, *Selected Writings of Thomas Jefferson,* p. 22.

18. Hudson, *Religion in America,* pp. 111–12.

19. From an address by Lyman Beecher in 1827, as quoted by Hudson, *Religion in America,* pp. 112–13.

20. Hudson, *Religion in America,* p. 112.

21. Quoted by Bellah, "American Civil Religion," p. 28.

22. The correlations of a two-item measure of civil religion ("God has chosen America to be a light to the world" and "God has blessed America more than other nations") with the voting measures are as follows: pro-choice on abortion, $r = -.42$, $p < .01$; civil liberties for homosexuals, $r = -.43$, $p < .01$); and pro–government spending, $r = -.38$, $p < .01$. For details on the voting measures see chapter 9.
23. The two-item measure correlates .39 ($p < .01$) with military expenditures and $-.40$ ($p < .01$) with foreign aid.
24. Robert Bellah, *Beyond Belief: Essays on Religion in a Post-Traditional World* (New York: Harper & Row, 1970).

Chapter 8

1. The number of items in each scale and scale reliabilities (coefficient *alpha*) are as follows:

Scale	Number of Items	Reliability
Agentic religion	7	.69
Communal religion	6	.60
Vertical religion	4	.81
Horizontal religion	3	.85
Restricting religion	9	.75
Releasing religion	5	.77
Comforting religion	3	.60
Challenging religion	3	.71
Evangelical religion	9	.78
Orthodoxy	5	.68
Symbolic	6	.73
Pro-Church	5	.74
Pro-Religion	4	.80

2. For an earlier measure of Vertical and Horizontal orientations, see James Davidson, "Glock's Model of Religious Commitment: Assessing Some Different Approaches and Results," *Review of Religious Research* 16 (Winter 1975): 83–93. For a discussion of the Comfort and Challenge dimensions, see Charles Y. Glock, Benjamin B. Ringer, and Earl R. Babbie, *To Comfort and to Challenge* (Berkeley and Los Angeles: University of California Press, 1967). The restricting and releasing themes are similar to the law and Gospel orientations identified in Strommen et al., *Study of Generations*.
3. David Bakan, *The Duality of Human Existence* (Chicago: Rand McNally, 1966).
4. The correlation between coders' ratings and interviewers' ratings is .60, $p < .001$.
5. There are substantial intercorrelations among the eight themes. For example, Agentic and Communal correlate $-.61$. Nonetheless, we find an important minority of members who score high or low on both. In order to permit these combinations we decided not to collapse each of the pairs of opposing themes into unidimensional scales. In later research, we will attempt to define the dimensions that underlie the eight themes. This work, which will depend on techniques such as factor analysis, necessitates a much larger sample of subjects than the eighty used in this study.

6. Cluster analysis is a multivariate procedure which locates groups or clusters of persons who (a) are similar to one another on the input variable, and (b) are maximally different on the same variables from all other groups or clusters of persons. The input variables were the thirteen multiple-item scales described earlier in this chapter.

7. For a description of what religious traditions were classified as liberal, mainline, and conservative, see the note to table 2-2.

Chapter 9

1. See, for example, Aage R. Clausen, *How Congressmen Decide* (New York: St. Martin's Press, 1973); James B. Kau and Paul H. Rubin, *Congressmen, Constituents, and Contributors* (Boston: Martinus Nijhoff Publishing, 1982); and John W. Kingdon, *Congressmen's Voting Decisions* (New York: Harper & Row, 1973).

2. The one exception to this conclusion is on the issue of abortion. See note 2, chapter 1, for appropriate studies.

3. See, for example, Michael Barone et al., *The Almanac of American Politics 1980*.

4. *Commentary*, September 1976.

5. Steven R. Weisman, "What Is a Conservative?" *New York Times Magazine*, August 31, 1980, pp. 12–15, 32–34.

6. The ADA voting scores for 1979 and 1980 were averaged.

7. For this analysis, we compared the 20 most liberal members to the 20 most conservative and computed *t*-tests for differences between the two means. In constructing table 9-1 we report only differences where the *t*-value has a probability less than .01. Because of the large number of variables in this study, we adopted this stringent level in order to minimize reporting chance relationships.

8. Table 9-2 is based on *t*-test values, comparing the 20 most liberal to the 20 most conservative members in the sample.

9. This voting analysis is available from The National Taxpayers Union, 325 Pennsylvania Ave., S.E., Washington, D.C. 20003.

10. ACA defines this measure as "for a private, competitive market and individual freedom of choice; against government interference by price fixing and controls." The measure is available from Americans for Constitutional Action, 955 L'Enfant Plaza North, S.W., Suite 1000, Washington, D.C. 20024.

11. ACA defines this as "for private ownership and control of the means of production and distribution."

12. The American Security Council 1980 Voting Index, Washington Communications Center, Boston, VA 22713.

13. Friends Committee on National Legislation, 245 Second St., N.E., Washington, D.C. 20002.

14. Bread for the World, 207 East Sixteenth St., New York, NY 10003.

15. National Women's Political Caucus, 1411 K St., N.W., Washington, D.C. 20005.

16. American Civil Liberties Union, 600 Pennsylvania Ave., S.E., Washington, D.C. 20003. We used only those votes which were not included in the abortion or hunger measures.

17. This analysis involved the thirty-two members who scored highest on the Orthodoxy scale.

18. Robert Wuthnow, "Religious Commitment and Conservatism: In Search of

an Elusive Relationship," in *Religion in Sociological Perspective: Essays on the Empirical Study of Religion*, ed. Charles Y. Glock (Belmont, Calif.: Wadsworth, 1973), p. 118.

19. The Wuthnow article provides an excellent review of this literature.
20. See note 2, chapter 1.
21. This point was made earlier. See note 1, this chapter.
22. Using a stepwise, multiple-regression procedure with four predictor variables (Agentic, Communal, Horizontal, Restricting), R^2 for the eight voting measures ranges from .31 (abortion) to .47 (pro–foreign assistance). These are highly notable R^2's. Nearly 50 percent of the variance on some voting measures ($R^2 = .47$ for foreign assistance, .46 for civil liberties, and .45 for military expenditures) can be accounted for by the four religion variables. The R^2 values using political party as the predictor range from .21 to .65. On civil liberties and foreign assistance, religion accounts for considerably more variance than does political party. On abortion, military expenditure, and hunger relief, religion and party account for similar amounts of variance. In a series of forthcoming professional journal articles, we will expand this discussion, and report the extent to which religion adds variance to that explained by the variance attributed to political orientation (using ADA and ACA measures).
23. One other problem deserves special mention. The eight voting measures we used were computed by lobbying groups who have a point of view. It is not known how well the votes these groups chose actually sample from the domain of votes that the voting indices are intended to measure. In later work we intend to empirically derive voting measures by using multivariate procedures like factor analysis to pinpoint relatively independent dimensions of voting.

Chapter 10

1. Falwell, *Listen America!* pp. 233–34.
2. Martin E. Marty, "Morality, Ethics, and the New Christian Right—Charisma or Compromise?" *Hastings Center Report*, August 4, 1981, p. 14.
3. Falwell, *Listen America!* p. 15.
4. James Robison, *Attack on the Family* (Wheaton, Ill.: Tyndale House Publishers, 1980), p. 130.
5. Ibid., p. 130.
6. Falwell, *Listen America!* p. 12.
7. This theme is prominent in the writings of New Christian Right leaders.
8. Lisa Myers, "Falwell Strives for Role as Kingmaker," *Washington Post*, Part 4 of a four-part series, July 8, 1980, p. 26.
9. For analyses of the composition of the New Christian Right, see Erling Jorstad, *The Politics of Moralism* (Minneapolis: Augsburg Publishing House, 1981); and Peggy L. Shriver, *The Bible Vote: Religion and the New Right* (New York: Pilgrim Press, 1981).
10. This voting report card is described in more detail in *Congressional Quarterly*, May 4, 1980, pp. 264–70.
11. Quoted in Jorstad, *Politics of Moralism*, p. 86, based on comments made by Jarmin on "Bill Moyers' Journal," September 29, 1980.
12. Jorstad, *Politics of Moralism*, p. 87.
13. See the *Minneapolis Star*, November 12, 1980, p. A1, for an interview with Terry Dolan of the National Conservative Political Action Committee.

14. See Jorstad, *Politics of Moralism,* and Shriver, *The Bible Vote,* for discussions of these criticisms.

15. David O. Moberg, *The Great Reversal: Evangelism versus Social Concern* (Philadelphia: J. B. Lippincott, 1972), p. 38.

16. Shriver, *The Bible Vote,* p. 34.

17. Daniel Yankelovich, "Stepchildren of the Moral Majority," *Psychology Today,* November 1981, p. 5.

18. For a discussion of what *evangelical* means, see Richard Quebedeaux, *The Young Evangelicals* (New York: Harper & Row, 1974); and Robert Webber and Donald Bloesch, *The Orthodox Evangelicals* (Nashville: Thomas Nelson, 1978). For an attempt to define the term empirically, see *Religion in America, 1981* (Princeton, N.J.: Gallup Organization and the Princeton Religious Research Center), p. 57.

19. Several members for whom data were missing on one of the first three criteria, but who otherwise met the criteria, were also included.

20. George Gallup estimates that 20 percent of American adults are evangelicals. See *Christianity Today,* December 21, 1979, p. 14.

21. The figures presented here on the political orientation of evangelicals are slightly different than those given in *Psychology Today,* December 1981. In the earlier report we examined the politics of those members who scored in the top one-third on the evangelical scale. In the present report we developed a system of criteria for selecting evangelicals. This, we suggest, is a more precise way to identify evangelicals.

22. *T*-tests were used to compare the means of eleven evangelical conservatives and nine evangelical liberals.

23. Mean differences reported here are all significant at the .001 level.

24. See Falwell, *Listen America!* for a description of the theological premises of the New Christian Right.

25. Falwell, *Listen America!* p. 57.

26. Ibid., p. 60.

27. Marty, "Morality, Ethics, and the New Christian Right," p. 17.

28. *Minneapolis Tribune,* September 16, 1981, p. 1.

Index